# NEW ENGLAND PAST

## Photographs 1880-1915

# NEW ENGL

## Photographs

Harry N. Abrams, Inc.,

selected and edited by Jane Sugden

text by Norman Kotker

# AND PAST

# 1880·1915

Publishers, New York

*Project Director:* Robert Morton
*Editor:* Joanne Greenspun
*Designer:* Carol Robson
*Captions:* Jane Sugden

LIBRARY OF CONGRESS CATALOGING IN PUBLICATION DATA

Sugden, Jane.
  New England past.

  1. New England — Description and travel — 1880 –
1915. 2. New England — Social life and customs.
I. Kotker, Norman. II. Title.
F9.S83  779'.9974041  80-20527
ISBN 0-8109-1357-7

Library of Congress Catalog Card Number: 80-20527

Illustrations © 1981 Harry N. Abrams, Inc.

Published in 1981 by Harry N. Abrams, Incorporated, New York
All rights reserved. No part of the contents of this book may be
reproduced without the written permission of the publishers

Printed and bound in Japan

*For my sister Claire*

# Contents

Vacationers pose at waterside in the Rangeley Lakes region of Maine.

On the front endpaper: in 1910 there were at least 1,888 automobiles
in Vermont, as the postman's license plate shows.

On the first page: two sisters stand for their portrait in Mansfield, Connecticut.

On the title pages: framing brick buildings are the elms of Woodstock, Vermont's Elm Street.

On the contents pages: oxen before the plow turn the rocky New England earth.

A few months after Parisians first saw the marvelous results of what the inventor Louis-Jacques-Mandé Daguerre called "a chemical and physical process which gives nature the ability to reproduce herself," New Englanders were able to admire photographs too. By 1840, daguerreotypes and a daguerreotype camera had been exhibited in Boston and Providence; within little more than a decade, over thirty professional photographers had opened businesses in Boston. They and their successors throughout New England took thousands of pictures that provide us with an extraordinary record of nineteenth-century life. Amateur photographers snapped thousands of photographs too, particularly after the maker of the Kodak hand camera introduced his invention to the public in 1888 with the guarantee, "You press the button, we do the rest."

A great many of these pictures survive in museums, libraries, and private collections throughout New England, and they provide us with a meticulously accurate picture of their times. Several hundred of the most interesting, characteristic, and beautiful of them have been selected for this book by Jane Sugden after extensive research; and they have been arranged by her to re-create the New England past, showing both the region's traditional life and the changes that were inexorably altering its character.

Life can't be neatly compartmentalized, but books have to be, and this book is divided into sections devoted to farming, factories, education, town life, resort life, and so on. Here, forever posed in one attitude like the figures of Keats's Grecian urn, factory workers work at their machines, farmers farm, and fishermen fish. But history is never immobile, as pictures are. Many factory workers also farmed and many farmers also fished for a living. The line between city and country was nowhere as distinct as it is now, after a plastic curtain of suburbs and shopping centers has descended to separate the two. When these pictures were taken, people moved from one environment to another with a democratic ease that we would find startling today. We have record of one small-town Connecticut boy, born in 1884, whose life could spread across every chapter of this book. He lived in a town, but he walked out into the country each morning to milk cows on the family farm, which his father had left years earlier to start a business in town. He attended a local, nationally important boarding school as a day student since his town had no high school of its own, and when he went off to college, he enjoyed lectures and fraternity parties in the winter and endured haying and harvesting in the summer. After graduation, he returned to his native town to live, but he took the trolley daily into an industrial city nearby to work on the bench at a brass factory, starting his successful business career at the bottom as so many New

England businessmen did. Like him, thousands of other New Englanders were at home in many worlds.

By the end of the nineteenth century—when most of these pictures were taken—New England farmers and fishermen had become almost quaint, and traditional Yankee life was disappearing, as those who treasured it most clearly realized. "We are vanishing into provincial obscurity. . . . The future is beyond us," the New England writer Barrett Wendell declared. New England, which had dominated so much of American history before the Civil War, no longer fully controlled even its own fate. It was becoming a colony of New York, as can be seen on the following pages in the pictures devoted to resort life and education. Although it is less visible in these photographs, the colonization was also taking place in agriculture, industry, and the fisheries. New England schoolchildren did learn that Boston was called the "hub of the universe"; that their ancestors had established the foundations for almost all of America's virtues; that Longfellow was theirs, along with Whittier and Emerson and Holmes and Samuel F. B. Morse and John Hancock and Paul Revere and Lexington and Concord and Thanksgiving and the "Battle Hymn of the Republic." As the nineteenth century reached its close, New Englanders increasingly came to idealize their past as a society where every citizen was virtuous and pious and life was quaint but terribly earnest. That realm—so imaginary it might well be called "Puritania"—never really existed the way they visualized it. But idealized or not, New England's traditional society was gone, or it was going fast. New Englanders were glad to be free of its restraints, but they mourned its passing. The region still had some economic power and its authors were still widely read, but the great days were over. "It is time that we perished," Brooks Adams, the descendant of two presidents, wrote to his brother Henry Adams. "The world is tired of us."

The pictures in this book present positive images in more ways than one, for the malaise that was overcoming New England at the time they were taken is hardly visible in them. The people shown have now perished, along with many of their traditions; the world they inhabited is gone. But their images survive thanks to "the mirror of memory," which is what that enthusiastic amateur photographer Oliver Wendell Holmes called the camera. "The very things which an artist would leave out or render imperfectly," Holmes wrote in the *Atlantic Monthly* in 1859, "the photograph takes infinite care with, and so renders its illusions perfect." On the following pages those perfect illusions appear with their million random details, the raw material of history, sharply focused and carefully composed though they are, the way history never is.

# I.

# RURAL LIFE

Above, piglets cuddle up by the stove in a farmhouse
at Norfolk, Connecticut.

On the preceding page, a turn-of-the-century village
with white-spired church and white clapboard houses nestles
in the hills of New Hampshire.

"Keep the sheep warm," the *Farmers' Almanac* advised farmers in January, 1882, when, not surprisingly, cold and frosty weather was predicted. "Weed out the strawberries," farmers were told in May, and in November, "House the cart and tools." "Idleness is the sepulchre of a living man," they were warned, and, apparently, the sepulchre of animals too since the almanac recommended that its readers "keep no more cats than will kill mice." New England farmers lived hard and close lives; everything and every moment was used. Old sheep that wouldn't last the winter—and sometimes diseased cows too—were slaughtered and sold to meat canners. (It was in the days before the pure food and drug act.) Old folks worked continually, the women knitting and cooking and sewing, and the men, no longer able to go outside to do heavy work, producing drumsticks and clothespins and embroidery hoops to be sold to a jobber in town, for there was an endless supply of wood that the strong younger men hauled in from the woodlot. The children worked ("An idle youth, a needy age," the almanac warned) and the animals worked too; horses, which have a normal life-span of thirty-five or forty years, were usually worn out after a dozen.

We've all seen it pictured—on kitchen calendars, in Currier and Ives prints, in the storybooks of our childhood—the beautiful New England farm. The house is white, the barn is red, the grass is green, and the cows are munching it. The farmer is harnessing his team and the farmer's wife is in the yard scattering feed to the chickens; the farmer's kids are swinging happily from a rope hung on a tree. It's the stuff fantasies are made of, but it was not a fantasy. It was real and often, despite the brutally hard work, it was very beautiful. There's an apple pie baking in the oven; you can tell something good is cooking because in those summery scenes smoke is coming out of the chimney. Beyond the farmhouse are the orchard, the meadow, and the deep tangled wild wood. The old oaken bucket hangs in the well.

To us it is something out of the past, a dim memory, in a landscape we would be happy to return to. But even in the past, in the decades after the Civil War, when these photographs were being taken, it was becoming a memory. The self-sufficient family farm, that stern but happy New England homestead where Hannah spun the wool and Silas cobbled the family's shoes, was obsolete by the end of the Civil War. Farmers who wanted properly fitting shoes went to the trouble of tanning the skin of the family cow and waiting until an itinerant cobbler came by to work it; but most people bought shoes that fit either foot (right and left lasts were a late development) from a store in town, and then broke them in. As late as the 1920s Calvin Coolidge delighted reporters and photographers by wearing a homespun farmer's smock while posing with a pitchfork. But most farmers bought woolens by the yard, either by mail or on a shopping trip to town.

By 1870 New England farming had become specialized. Farm products were shipped to market, and the farmer and his wife lived in a cash economy. In the last decades of the nineteenth century the typical New England farmer probably spent his time not very romantically, planting onions on mucky bottomlands or packing peaches to ship to New York or—if in Middlesex County, Massachusetts, then one of the nation's most profitable agricultural counties and now an epitome of the suburban dream with its engineering plants and ranch houses—growing lettuce and cucumbers under glass to ship to the Boston market.

Of course, there were many relics of the traditional way of life. New England has always been two lands: northwest and southeast, the hill country and the coastal plain with river valleys that extend inward from it. If you start on Connecticut's western border, a few miles north of where the New York commuter trains stop at Danbury, and draw a line northeastward toward Penobscot Bay, you'll have a rough approximation of the boundary line between the two lands. Northwest of that line was pioneer country, unsafe until the Indians were tamed at the end of the French and Indian Wars in 1763. There, where the snow lay deep on the roads all winter so that families had to travel to church by sleigh and farmwives served baked beans on Saturday night for the original reason—because beans could be reheated on Sunday without breaking the Biblical sabbath commandment "Thou shalt not do any work"— a few farmers still sustained themselves by old-fashioned subsistence farming well into the nineteenth century.

In this primitive and hilly country—still the least settled part of New England and the delight of tourists and city people going back to the land—men couldn't combine farming with fishing as they did along the Maine coast; they couldn't go into town and work part time in factories as so many southern New Hampshire farmers did. They were too far from markets to be able to make much of a profit sending their cash crops to the city. But still most of them shipped out butter and lard, wool and cider, cattle or meat and hides, and maple syrup to be used for sweetening plugs of chewing tobacco. (There wasn't much call for maple sugar; once Louisiana cane sugar became available again after the Civil War, the bottom dropped out of the maple sugar market.) But farmers stuck it out, picturesquely, just scraping by, or they packed up and left altogether. A great many left.

Because it was almost unendurably hard to stay. A glance at the diaries kept with Puritan industry shows what their days were like. On January 1, 1873, one New Hampshire farmwife recorded: "Cooked all day." On January 2 she churned and on January 3 she sewed. She spent January 8 trying lard and cutting sausage meat; and then in the evening, she ground the sausage meat. This means that outside in the barnyard that week her husband had slaughtered a hog or two and scalded off the bristles and butchered the hog and set hams and bacon in the smokehouse to cure and built the smokehouse fire and regulated it daily along with doing his other chores. On January 14 the farmwife dressed nine chickens, churned butter, and baked thirteen pies—all this plus washing the floor every other day, cooking, doing dishes, frying donuts by the peck, raising children and sending them off to school, tending fires and, not least, writing in her diary.

We've all seen sentimental pictures of the farmer's Thanksgiving, with the fire in the fireplace and the candles on the mantelpiece and the pies and turkey on the table. But we don't remember the blood in the barnyard before Thanksgiving, the slaughter of the turkey on the chop log, the plucking of its carcass. Nor do we remember the smell of tallow being rendered to make the candles ("Dipped sixty dozen candles today," one diary entry reads); or the labor required to haul and chop wood for the blazing fire; or the long chilly ride to church; or the even longer and chillier Thanksgiving sermon with the children quarreling to see whose turn it was to sit on the comfortable seat next to mother and the family's tin foot stove with its burning coals.

It was very unromantic, as life usually is. It could be terribly cold in the winter, so cold that the Christmas tree had to be set up in the kitchen because the front parlor couldn't be made warm enough. The snow was always three or four feet deep, and strange, frightening noises were heard on winter nights as trees burst from frost with a sound like a cannon. The work was endless. In the winter it was dark when the farmer woke his hired man and then went out to milk the cows, and it was still dark when he came back into the house to have his breakfast at seven. Then he hauled his milk to the cheese factory if he was fortunate enough to live near a neighbor enterprising enough to set one up. But his main winter task was in the woodlot, cutting wood day after day and hauling it on a homemade sledge down through the snowdrifts to the woodshed or the sugarhouse. Some of the wood might be used for a small home factory with one shift on winter evenings, producing paintbrush handles or coat hangers or any number of other small, easily transportable and saleable items. But most of it found its way into the woodshed, where morning and evening it was brought inside the house by the farmer's son, whose job it was to fill the woodbox by the stove so that the peck of donuts could be fried and the heat ascend through a grate in the ceiling to warm a chilly bedroom upstairs.

During the spring the main tasks involved skill as much as strength — mending walls whose stones had been dislodged by the ice and snow, and sugaring off. This meant burning the pith out of sumac wood to make new spouts for tapping the maple trees, rehooping and washing the sap buckets, setting the buckets, and tapping the sap. It meant guiding a reluctant horse, with a tub into which the buckets were emptied dragging behind him, from tree to tree through the snow and mud and then down to the sugarhouse. There the fire had to be tended day after day for weeks on end while the sap boiled until it was ready and it was time for the sugar party, when boys and girls gathered to boil eggs in the syrup and bake potatoes in the ashes under the evaporator. Finally the big day came when the farmer and the hired man got the plow and harrow ready, after they had milked the cows and before they had eaten breakfast. The seed had already been sorted and the potatoes had been sliced for planting, and it was time for the farmer's classic task to begin: plow the fields behind a team of horses or trudging oxen; harrow; plant the seeds; and then finally hoe a hill of dirt over the seeds to cover them.

And then during the hottest time of year came haying, with the scythes sharpened and the hay cut and then spread with pitchforks in the field to dry in the July sun and turned to dry again the next day. "Mighty hot for hayin'," people complained, but they complained even more if a sudden shower broke the summer heat because that meant more work. Then the dry hay was raked into windrows to be stacked and hauled off, load by load, and "mowed away" in the haymow, where the children could hang a swing from the barn rafters and safely jump into the hay. Hay was stacked throughout the barn, leaving only a narrow passageway along which the farmer could walk in winter on his way to milk the cows. As the winter progressed, the passageway grew wider until by spring no more hay was left.

In the autumn came the work of the harvest. The hayfields had been fertilized with newfangled "chemical manures" which gave better results than manure made in the barnyard. The barn was full, corn was in the corncrib, apples were in their barrels, the preserves had been put up, and the potatoes, onions, turnips, and carrots were stashed away. The cows were led into the barn for the winter, and the children were led into the district schoolhouse. It was time for the cold season to set in with its terrible isolation.

As the decades went by, life on the hill farms became more and more isolated. True, by the 1880s almost every town in Vermont and New Hampshire was within a dozen miles of a railroad, although they were often difficult miles. True, social opportunities increased. State agricultural boards ran institutes where farmers learned about milk testing or modern fertilizers; and the Grange, where members chatted about fertilizers and neighbors debated the relative merits of raising sheep or cattle, became increasingly active. There were skating and sleighriding and bobsledding for the children, and sliding down the snow-covered roofs of saltbox houses. There were the village store and post office for visiting from time to time. But as more and more people abandoned farms to move to town or to new lands out West, social life became more meager. Despite the warning published in a New Hampshire magazine, the *Farmer's Monthly Visitor*, that those who moved West would find "the social, moral, literary, and religious privileges are there much less," young people moved westward in droves. What the *Farmer's Monthly Visitor* called "the pecuniary view" prevailed. The hill country which had been settled only toward the end of the eighteenth century had become sparsely populated again by the end of the nineteenth, and farms that had been laboriously cleared were allowed to revert to woodland. Vermont was especially hard hit. Fewer than half of the soldiers who went off to fight in the Civil War returned home. They preferred to move to the rich and free grainlands of the West.

Farmers and their families were constantly exposed to the blandishments of the West. The illustrated magazines that they read in the evenings—those *Pictorials* and *Illustrated Monthlies*, and the local *Gazettes* and *Eagles*—informed them that bountiful grainlands, easy to farm, were to be had for the asking out West. In 1880 more natives of Vermont lived outside the state than in it. Although the population of the three southern New England states increased by 88 percent in the next decade, the population of Vermont increased by a scanty 7 percent. In the farming towns a new tradition arose called Old Home Week, when emigrants and their children returned to check the old homestead and make sure that the roof hadn't caved in, to eat bean suppers, compete in pie-eating contests, listen to speeches, and, if they had become rich, endow the old town with a library or a church organ. By the beginning of the twentieth century, Massachusetts and the northern New England states were publishing lists of abandoned hill country farms that were for sale. In 1910, these sold for around ten dollars an acre, when good bottomland in the river valleys was selling for forty or fifty times that amount. The farms were bought by summer people from New York or the New England cities or by immigrants—Poles, French Canadians, or a smattering of Irish and Italians—although not too many immigrants farmed. Most of them had left Europe to escape a poverty-stricken rural life.

The depopulation frightened people, for increasing isolation encouraged inbreeding. "What has happened in the hill country of Alabama and Tennessee is happening in the hill country of New England," one writer complained in the *Atlantic*

*Monthly* in 1899. "We are evolving a race of poor whites." A sociological study of twenty-one towns in southeastern Vermont found an astonishingly high incidence of prostitution and illegitimacy. Peyton Place was being born.

The exodus from the hill farms had been hastened by the decline in sheep and cattle raising, which had once been mainstays of the economy. Earlier in the nineteenth century as many as five thousand sheep and eight thousand cattle would enter Boston's livestock market from northern New England daily. Even around 1880, during the heyday of the Chisholm Trail, when cowboys annually drove thousands of longhorns north from Texas to the railroad, drovers were still taking hundreds of cattle down through New England main streets, southward along the Connecticut River. Sheep raising had once been highly profitable but after the tariff on foreign wool was lifted in 1883, Massachusetts textile manufacturers could import wool from Australia more cheaply than from Vermont and Maine. Massachusetts shoe factories could buy Western hides for less than it cost to buy hides tanned right in New England. Although breeding Merino sheep remained lucrative because sheep developed especially thick fleece in Vermont, the number of sheep in that state fell by about 25 percent in the decade after 1870. Oats, wheat, and other grain had been major agricultural products, but eventually it became cheaper to buy grain from the West than to grow it. In an attempt to make ends meet, many farmers cut down their apple orchards and turned the land to other uses; the Temperance Movement had cut the demand for hard cider, which had once been a staple drink of New England. By the 1880s there was widespread farm depression.

But the economic picture was not entirely bleak. There were still prosperous farms. Outside all the major cities, tracts of land were profitably devoted to truck farming. In the Connecticut Valley, cigar-leaf tobacco growers made good money and imported horse manure from the streets of New York to fertilize their fields. New agricultural specialties arose. Poultry raising became a big industry, and Rhode Island Reds for breeding sold for as much as one hundred dollars each. The building of the Bangor and Aroostook Railroad in the 1890s opened an enormous fertile acreage of sandy loam in northern Maine where farmers, among them many Swedish immigrants who weren't scared away by the cold and the short growing season, bought land and planted potatoes. Peach orchards covered hillsides in Connecticut (a south-facing slope was best, farmers were advised, with plenty of space between the trees so that air could circulate), and by 1911 Connecticut was the country's leading peach-growing state.

But most important was milk. Of course, farmers fortunate enough to live near a town had always peddled milk in town, but in isolated northern New England milk had to be turned into cheese or butter before it would bring in cash. Around 1900 Vermont farmers formed a cooperative to ship milk to Boston; sometimes at the cooperative dairy, cream was separated out for shipping and the skim milk was returned to the farmer to feed to the pigs; but whether whole milk or cream was shipped, the farmer made money, and in Boston the price of milk went up. A special milk train began running from Vermont to Boston, and the entire state became hooked into the Boston milkshed. By 1900 dairying supported half the farms in Vermont, a third of those in New Hampshire, and more than a fourth in Maine, and it supported them well.

Nor was the social picture entirely bleak. A class of poor whites was developing (rural blacks, poor or rich, were few and far between except in southern Rhode Island, which had had a plantation economy in colonial times), but the rural Yankee virtues and customs survived. Most farm families went to church every Sunday. Their children went to school at least some of the time, and a few of the brightest boys even scraped together enough money to go to college. Isolation forced people to find occasions to socialize whenever possible. There actually *were* husking bees where any boy who found a red ear of corn could kiss the girl of his choice; and singing bees; and candy pulls. On winter evenings, if the weather was clear, farm boys could walk or sleigh into town for amusement. There were games of checkers and backgammon, and the *Farmers' Almanac* carried pages of puzzles and riddles for "Winter Evening Amusements." The minister came to call, even in bad weather; that was part of his job. In southeastern Massachusetts, sunbonneted girls harvesting cranberries in the bogs chatted as much as they worked, and in southern New England townspeople could even take the trolley out to the country to help with the harvest in the fall.

One of the greatest pleasures in every New England rural town was the annual day-long town meeting, which usually took place in early spring. There the children could pick up a few extra pennies by selling popcorn balls and apples to their fellow citizens; the women could visit with each other as they prepared the meal of baked beans and brown bread, coffee and donuts (they didn't participate otherwise); and the men could hold forth informing each other of what should and should not be done and deliberating over each vote for selectman or town clerk.

Above all, there were the agricultural fairs, local and countywide, which had originated in Berkshire County, Massachusetts, early in the nineteenth century and had become an American institution. There were plowing contests and ox-hauling contests with teams of oxen pulling at enormous blocks of granite. There was a prize for the most beautiful pumpkin, worthy of becoming Cinderella's coach. There were competitions in quilts and maple syrup and butter and livestock, while chickens strutted about competing for beauty prizes. The bigger fairs attracted throngs, and railroads sometimes offered visitors half-fare tickets and carried livestock for show free of charge (at the owner's risk it must be added; the railroad management accepted no responsibility for damage). The smaller fairs attracted people from just a few neighboring towns, but the program was the same. In later years, the summer people who were buying up some of the prettier abandoned farms were invited to judge the pies, quilts, and displays, although not the livestock, which required a professional eye. As outsiders, they wouldn't play favorites.

That rural life has not entirely disappeared. There are still about twenty-five thousand farms in New England with more than one hundred thousand people living on them. Milk, poultry, fruit, tobacco, and potatoes are still major crops. The town and county fairs survive, although the hand-carpentered whirlarounds on which the farm children used to ride have been stored in barns, replaced by concessionaires' machines. The churches—now there is often only one in rural towns instead of two or three—still draw people on Sundays, and the minister still goes calling from farm to farm. Newspapers in rural areas still report Grange activities and the price of cattle and advertise hay and pigs for sale. Farmers still get up uncomfortably early to milk their cows, which nowadays involves plugging the cows into a milking machine. Much of what is gone never to return is, paradoxically, still around, though at farm museums and villages scattered throughout New England. There suburb-bred college graduates, dressed up in old costumes, plow and hoe and sheep-shear and chop wood, on stage as it were, for the edification and amusement of the television generation.

Hazel True, a Maine farmgirl, feeds the family chickens.

Farm houses throughout New England
were sheathed against wind and rain in clapboard.


Above, before their Connecticut home, the kids mount up for an ox-cart ride.
At right are two proud western Massachusetts families.


On the preceding pages is a Maine hill farm with ample barns.

Midsummer, in Maine as elsewhere, meant haying time.

The soil of northern Maine,
ideal for growing potatoes, produced some whoppers.

A Massachusetts man harvests greenhouse cucumbers for the city market.

Workers in a western Massachusetts orchard display a fine haul of peaches.

Near York, Maine, above, two sheep shearers and their helper produce the first crop of the year —spring wool.

Above, the womenfolk and a farmhand pitch in on laundry day
at the Marsh farm in Madison, Connecticut.

At right, a farm wife churns butter
in the isolated mountain town of Kingfield, Maine.

The timber frames of New England post-and-beam built barns
were so heavy that sections were assembled on the ground
and then "raised" by all the friends and neighbors
a farmer could muster. Above, a wall goes up.

At right, in Killingworth, Connecticut,
a family named Marcinek, probably Polish immigrants,
poses in the frame of their newly raised barn.
Farmers usually rewarded their helpers with a big feed
when the new building was topped out.

New England farmers had a cash crop in winter—ice. The icehouse near York, Maine, above, was right at pond side. Near Putney, Vermont (at right), ice was cut in the river.

Tradesmen in farm communities invariably included a miller and a blacksmith.

In the Connecticut town of Norfolk,
a well-equipped and amply assisted farrier shoes a white horse.

At left, a bearded farmer holds a sack of flour inside a gristmill
in Old Mystic, Connecticut.

Even small country towns usually could support one merchant who
sold groceries, dry goods, farm implements, and shoes, and doubled as a postmaster.
The general store above was in Vermont.


At top right, in Cary, Maine,
townsfolk assemble on a wooden sidewalk in front of their provisioner's.


Bottom right, in Connecticut a more prosperous shop featured a soda fountain.

One-room schoolhouses,
where children of various ages learned
their three Rs, were the rule in rural towns.


The schoolhouse above served Stowe, Vermont.


In 1902, the children
of Peacham, Vermont, at right, studied beneath
the crossed flags of the United States and Cuba,
the island which they learned
was recently won from Spain and
then granted independence.

When not in school, farm children had chores;
above, Vermont youngsters show they know all about making maple sugar.

In the summer an itinerant organ grinder delights (and mystifies) children
in Scituate, Massachusetts.

Deerfield, Massachusetts, women make baskets on a neighbor's porch.

Some of the ladies of Boothbay Harbor,
Maine gather for a quilting bee in the town's
Masonic Hall, stitching industriously
under protection of the letter G,
which stands for God.

In Deerfield, Massachusetts,
a woman and her children prepare
Christmas wreaths for holiday decoration.

Above, on the Fourth of July a Vermont man amazed his townsfolk
with a demonstration of tightrope walking.


Traveling entertainers appeared everywhere, even in places as remote
as Wilton in western Maine, top right,
where a dancing bear performs in the village square.


Below, at right, a pair of homegrown fiddlers in Vermont
competes for the photographer's attention with a brace of hunting dogs
and a music lover.

Communal activities in small towns served social as well as economic functions.

Above and at lower left are two Vermont auctions, a familiar and often amusing method of exchanging property.

At left, above, Maine farm families gather for a husking bee.

Every country fair had its showoffs, even in sober New England.

At left, a prize-winning pumpkin merits serious attention at Connecticut's Danbury Fair.
Above, in Biddeford, Maine, where a lady seems to think they ought to know better,
three wags model the latest in aprons.

The annual Valley Fair in Brattleboro, Vermont, above,
had large permanent fair buildings,
and a real ferris wheel.

Fairs at Sturbridge, Massachusetts, below,
and Berlin, Connecticut, right, were smaller, but they too
had their diversions—among them
a balloon and a primitive "tilt-a-whirl" ride.

In Tunbridge, Vermont, the fairground,
with its racetrack, amusements, food stalls,
and livestock displays, occupied
one of the few level stretches in town.
At center is the ubiquitous
photographer's tent, where for a few cents
Aunt Sarah was immortalized.

# II.

# FISHERMEN, WOODSMEN, QUARRYMEN

A bearded lobsterman works in his dory at Annisquam on Cape Ann in Massachusetts.

In 1784 the Massachusetts legislature voted to "hang the representation of a codfish in the room where the House sit, as a memorial of the importance of the codfishery to the welfare of the Commonwealth." More than a century later, when the Massachusetts statehouse was remodeled, the sacred cod was lowered, wrapped in an American flag, placed on a bier, and solemnly carried to the new chamber of the House of Representatives. When the procession entered the chamber, the members arose, applauding, and the totem was placed on a table in front of the speaker's chair, until it could be hung high above the legislators' seats to oversee their deliberations.

"The land is full of Gods good blessings," one of the first explorers of New England had written, "so is the Sea replenished with a great abundance of excellent fish." The explorer, who visited New England in 1603, sailed down the coast from Maine to Plymouth harbor. A seaman from the British port of Bristol, he and his mates had stuck close to the coast; had they penetrated inland, they would have seen that God's good blessings were there too. Alewives, shad, and salmon ran the plentiful rivers. Trees grew everywhere, astonishingly tall, a wonderful sight to the Englishmen who finally settled the land; their own long-inhabited country, like all of Western Europe, had little forest left. There was bog iron in the marshes and, in time, the treasures that could be mined and quarried from the earth would bring New England much wealth.

But of all God's blessings, it was the fish that impressed the English most. "Cods sufficient to lade many ships . . . Seales to make oil withall, Mullets, Turbuts, Mackerels, Herrings, Lobsters, Crevises, and Muscels with ragged Pearles in them." For the long centuries before the tourists came to swallow the bait of the picturesque, fisheries sustained the economy of much of the New England coast. The southern ports —New London and Mystic, New Bedford and Nantucket—grew rich on the oil they obtained from sealing and whaling. The ports farther north—Provincetown, Marblehead, Gloucester, and the dozens of seaside villages of Maine—never grew rich from fishing; but at least their inhabitants never lacked for chowders to keep their bellies full.

New England was almost the only part of the United States where fishing was commercially significant before the Civil War. Long after the war was over, fisheries remained very important. All along the coast were tryhouses for boiling down oil from menhaden, which New Englanders called porgy. Porgy oil was less glamorous than whale oil, but it brought in more money annually. There were smokehouses, fueled by birch or driftwood, where salted herring by the thousands hung for weeks to be cured. There were fish flakes, or racks, along the beaches where cod, eviscerated and filleted, were set out to dry just as the Indians had dried them. There were great gray-shingled, barnlike canneries located on wharves, where boys and girls worked at cutting tables, skillfully, with one swipe of a knife, separating the head and entrails from young herring which would be canned and sold to the public as "sardines." Some towns specialized in herring, some in cod, and some in mackerel; and some years the catch was good but many years it was meager. And always the work was hard and dangerous.

Danger was one of the prices the fisherman paid for his independence, for the fisherman was as free as the farmer and far freer than his neighbor who had gone to work in the mills. (Many fishermen, though, managed to combine two or all three of these occupations.) Every man on a fishing boat had a financial interest in the catch but he had to work hard for it, no matter what sort of catch he was after. When out seining for mackerel, the first gang of the crew ate breakfast by 3:30 A.M. because dawn was one of the best times for catching mackerel. When the lookout at the masthead called out "school!" the entire crew tumbled overboard into the seine boat, along with the captain, leaving the cook, who had been awake since 2:30, in charge of the ship. The seine, a great net with a purse string to draw it shut, was cast around the school — it took strong men to cast it far enough — and then the purse string was drawn. The netted fish were hauled into the seine boat, and then hauled again onto the deck of the fishing boat, where they were split, gutted, and salted, or packed into barrels between layers of chipped ice. On a cold day on the high seas it was chilly work.

On a trawler winter-fishing for cod — winter-caught fish commanded higher prices — men spent hours on deck each day cutting the frozen herring that was used for bait and uncoiling and recoiling the mile-long trawl line to which they attached it. The trawl lines were taken into two-man dories, weighted so that they would sink, let out, and then laboriously hauled in again by one of the dorymen, while his mate unhooked the fish and rebaited and recoiled the trawl to get it ready for the next haul. It was not very pleasant to be out in a dory on a foggy winter evening rowing toward where you thought your trawler might be and hoping you'd find it or that it would find you.

Aboard the trawler again, the dorymen set to work in teams, assembly-line style, decapitating, splitting, and gutting the cod and filling a barrel with livers to be made into cod-liver oil, that vile-tasting tonic that sickened generations of American children to whom it was supposed to bring health. ("Don't use it," pediatricians now warn; synthetic vitamins are better and more palatable.) If the catch was hake or haddock, it was sold as cod anyway. Once it was dried for the export market, customers didn't know the difference; but at home, on shore, the fishermen's wives knew. They preferred cod for making their fish chowders, with haddock an acceptable second, and hake a poor third.

Whaling could be an even more difficult and dangerous occupation. No cod or mackerel ever overturned a fishing dory or rammed through it the way whales upended whaleboats. Whalers in the South Seas nervously feared encountering cannibals when they went ashore for water. In northern seas there was danger of hitting a great white iceberg, or of being crushed by Arctic ice as thirty-three New England whaling vessels were in 1871. But there were advantages in whaling, most notably the immense profits derived from successful voyages, which paid for Nantucket mansions almost as splendid as those the rich China-trade sea captains built in Salem. Another advantage was getting to see the tourist sights—performances by bare-breasted dancing girls on the South Sea islands and jaunts ashore in Chile or Zanzibar. Whaling voyages could last for years, and whalemen, whaling captains at least, could take their wives, children, and pets along to breathe both the healthy sea air and the terrible fumes from the on-deck tryworks, where blubber fires fueled vats of boiling blubber while the crew skimmed off whale oil. One eight-year-old New Bedford girl on a Pacific whaling voyage in 1870 wrote home to her grandmother: "We went to an island named Ohitahoo and staid eight days. We went to the Queen's palace and she made a feast for us. Mama was the first white woman that ever was on the island. . . . Papa has taken sperm whales that made 83 barrels. . . . Lots of kisses from your dear Laura."

By the time dear Laura was grown up, the harbor at New Bedford was filled with dozens of idle, dismantled whalers. There was still a trade in whalebone, which was used for corset stays, but the market for whale oil had vanished, as gas, kerosene, and then electric lamps replaced whale-oil lamps. The fishing industry in Maine declined too. After 1880 the herring catch dwindled, and the sardine canneries along the Maine coast were devoted more and more to canning blueberries and vegetables. Canadians were given the right to sell their fish duty-free in the United States, and Maine fishermen had trouble meeting their competition. More competition came when railroad cars made it possible for midwesterners and easterners to buy West Coast salmon instead of New England fish. Fewer trips were made to the waters of Iceland and Greenland in search of halibut, fish so enormous that once they were landed on deck they had to be stunned with a mallet like steers in the Chicago stockyards. Besides, the summer people were coming. Fishermen and their families found it more profitable and infinitely less toilsome to cater to them, tending their houses and boats, and fishing inshore in summer to supply them with food rather than going out to the Grand Banks in winter. Many of the unsightly canneries at the end of the town wharves were torn down, to be replaced by boathouses and yacht clubs. After 1900 almost all the ports in Maine had abandoned Grand Banks fishing. Increasingly, New England fishing centered around Gloucester and Boston.

The Maine lobster industry survived though. It was relatively easy and profitable work pulling in lobster pots once a day. Lobsters, canned or shipped on ice to Boston and New York, brought good prices. But by 1905 the most valuable seafood gathered in New England was not cod or haddock brought into Gloucester or to the Boston Fish Pier. Surprisingly, it was Connecticut seafood—oysters which were sent directly to the fish markets of New York and then downed on the half shell, a dozen or two at a sitting, by the patrons of fashionable restaurants and bars.

Although the "great abundance of excellent fish" was not always abundant enough, New England continued to enjoy God's other good blessings. With immense stretches of forest, Maine, upper New Hampshire, and northeastern Vermont were logging country, where woodsmen tough as nails axed down the white pine and spruce that stretched for hundreds of miles across the northern hillsides. In many ways, lumbering was even harder work than fishing, and New England woodsmen lived more picturesque lives than did fishermen, although it was the fishermen who attracted most of what we would now call media attention. Woodsmen drank tablespoons of kerosene from time to time as a pick-me-up and dipped their chafed feet into tubs of lard each morning to help get their woolen stockings on.

Every winter, scouts in pairs snowshoed through the woods to find the great stands of timber which would be cut down the next season. Bosses rounded up work gangs in the rowdy lumber towns of Berlin, New Hampshire, and Bangor, Maine—French Canadians, Indians, Nova Scotians, Yankees, and Prince Edward Islanders, who always wore long white woolen underwear knitted by their mothers. Other lumbermen wore red underwear and shirts in the belief that they were warmer, and for the same reason they wore beards. In later years Finns joined the work crews. They were as tough as the other lumbermen except for one effete habit: they insisted on taking baths. But they won the respect of their fellow woodsmen by the way they bathed —in log saunas out of which they leaped stark naked to roll in the snow.

Each autumn these gangs traveled upriver to the logging camps, carrying all their possessions in satchels made of flour sacks tied together at the corners. There they built their winter bunkhouses out of logs cut at the site, filling in the drafty cracks with moss or mud. Before the snows set in they labored to clean out the stream they were planning to send their logs down, lugging out boulders and driftwood and clearing snags that might cause logjams in the spring. They cut logging roads up to the stand of pine or spruce they were aiming at (in later years, as the pine was used up, spruce was cut increasingly; hardwoods were ignored because the mills weren't powerful enough to pulp them); and they oiled the edges of their axes with lubricated whetstones to keep them sharp enough to shave with. Each morning they went out into the woods in three-man chopping crews to cut down first the trees that would make fifty-foot logs and then smaller trees, some so skimpy they were as thin around as an overweight logger; and when they found a cluster of wood ants hibernating in a pine tree they gobbled them down, claiming that they tasted like cranberries. Wood ants provided them with a convenient snack while they waited for the cook to bring out buckets of pork and beans or pea soup for their luncheon picnic in the woods.

The trees were cut so that they fell toward the logging road, where they could be loaded easily onto a sled to be skidded downhill. One man cut the limbs off the fallen trees. Then, in January, when the ice set in, the logs were loaded onto the sled for the tough ride along the ice down to the side of the stream. That job had to wait for the coldest part of the winter. Each night, after oxen or horses had hauled their sledloads of logs down to the side of the stream, a crew went uphill again with a barrel full of water to sprinkle the skid road to make sure it was icy enough for the logs to travel down the next day. Before the sprinkler crew could go off to bed, they had to rub down the legs of their oxen to get the ice off.

Then it was back to the dubious comforts of camp. At least it was warmer there, unless a logger decided to strip off his underwear and boil it on the stove to kill off the lice. Lice provided entertainment of a sort. Two of them, caught and trapped on a creased piece of newspaper, were pitted against each other and fought to the death. More entertainment came from dancing to the music of a fiddler. There was always one in camp. The French Canadians (unblushingly called Canucks) were the best dancers, performing solo jigs that had come over from France as *gigues* with their ancestors in the seventeenth century. The woodsmen ate pork and beans three times a day, gingerbread and molasses and Aroostook potatoes, and, unless the logging boss had had foresight enough to have a vegetable garden planted at the site the previous spring, vegetables hauled all the way from town.

When the ice broke in March, it was time for the drive downriver. "When the drive comes down," one loggers' song went, "Oh, it's then we're paid our money and it's then we own the town! And the gutters run with whiskey when the shanty boys so frisky set their boot calks in the sidewalks when the drive is down." They were indeed frisky. After the trip downriver—breaking up logjams, dislodging logs caught in the banks of a river, poling through shallows, and painfully towing immense booms across lakes—they deserved a little vacation. Around the time of the Civil War and even afterward, Bangor, with its whorehouses and saloons, was as wild as any cow town or mining town out West. It was not the New England of the schoolteachers, poets, and ministers.

The longest annual log drive went from the hills of Vermont and New Hampshire down the Connecticut River to Massachusetts. Sometimes the drive was a hundred miles long. Logs from the Ammonoosuc in New Hampshire and the tributaries of the White River in Vermont would end up boomed in the Oxbow of the Connecticut River at Northampton, where Smith College girls could stroll down a civilized hillside to peer at the loggers. The logs would be chewed up and pulped for the insatiable mills of Holyoke, "the Paper City," just to the south. Holyoke was another rough-and-tumble town, but unlike the raw Maine paper towns which produced only wrapping paper and newsprint, it more classily specialized in writing paper and book paper. A few miles west, Dalton, in the Massachusetts Berkshires, was classiest of all. The paper it manufactured went into United States bank notes.

Mining and quarrying were much tamer, but they too were among God's blessings on New England. There was granite almost everywhere, especially along the seashore, and inland there were marble and slate. In the 1880s one of the country's richest copper mines was in Bristol, Connecticut. From the town of Portland on the lower reaches of the Connecticut River, brownstone was barged to Long Island Sound and then over to Manhattan and Brooklyn to make those cities' characteristic brownstone row houses. By 1896 Portland had the nation's largest stonecutting establishment. Quincy granite had been famous since the days when the nation's first railroad had been constructed to transport it down to a quay from which it could be shipped north for the building of the Bunker Hill Monument. There was a Rockport shipping out granite in Maine, and a Rockport shipping out granite in Massachusetts. Some cities like Fall River were practically built of local granite; house foundations, mills, and the city hall rose from rock quarried at the site. Scandinavian quarrymen came to work along the Maine coast and in Vermont, miners from Wales, where slate deposits had been worked even in Roman times, brought their skills to the slate mines. In their new home, they worshiped at their own churches, where services were entirely in Welsh.

New England produced paving stones, seawalls, and hitching posts, and stone for factories and churches, statehouses, and customhouses. All along the western border, from Connecticut to Canada, there was a rich vein of marble which had been quarried since the eighteenth century. Visiting Italians from the land of Michelangelo maintained that it was as fine as the marble of Carrara. In Connecticut, marble quarrying began in a section of the town of Washington appropriately called Marbledale; farther north another town provided marble for the Connecticut statehouse. Over the border in the Massachusetts Berkshires, marble was quarried and hauled across the hills to the Hudson to be shipped downriver to make New York's City Hall. When the U.S. Capitol was being enlarged in 1867, the marble for it came from the Berkshires.

But Vermont was the major marble state. In 1885 it could boast an acre-size marble quarry with walls over a hundred feet high, where channeling machines sawed furrows into the stone day and night. This quarry had more than five hundred workmen—Yankees, Canadians, immigrants from all parts of the British Isles, and Italians with their long tradition of marble quarrying. If the Italians were homesick (by 1900 there were two thousand of them in the state's quarrying centers) they could find solace in the fact that one marble site was renamed Florence in honor of their homeland's artistic center. Vermont could also boast of a mountain made completely of marble, protected by a thin cap of slate. And above all it could boast of its automatic production in a stonecutting mill that won a government contract for more than a quarter million tombstones for Civil War veterans. These were produced by an ingenious device that covered each tombstone with an iron facing and then sandblasted it in such a way as to display for eternity, in raised letters, the deceased veteran's name, regiment, and rank.

Houses for the living were important, of course, and many Vermont houses still have marble lintels and thresholds. But increasingly New England quarrying moved toward the business of supplying houses for the dead. Marble gravestones had been popular in the nineteenth century, but as the decades went on, granite, more solid than marble, more solid even than life itself, was used more frequently. If they were fortunate enough to die on land, Maine fishermen found their final resting place under local granite, as did the Maine woodsmen, although their monuments tended to be smaller and cheaper, for woodsmen all too often blew their money; they didn't take it with them. The fishermen of Gloucester and the whalers of New Bedford lay under Quincy granite, and the miners of Vermont were interred under stone—granite or marble—that they may very well have quarried themselves.

Swampscott, Massachusetts fishermen display their catch and gear.

Poling his boat with an oar, a Maine lobsterman seeks deeper water to set his "pots."

At right, at day's end, a lobsterman carries his sail and a basket of catch from his beached boat.

At Newport, two Rhode Island fishermen stow their nets
within sight of the mansions of the summer people.

Fishermen in southern Massachusetts ports sometimes trapped herring
in fish weirs, as the Indians had done. This weir was near Hyannis on Cape Cod.

A Maine fisherman
rakes for clams at low tide.

New Bedford, Massachusetts fishermen net mackerel.

Even on the beach, work continues in an offshore fishing dory.

Sightseers visit the herring storage pens at Mattapoisett,
near New Bedford, Massachusetts.

At Gloucester, Massachusetts,
dock workers prepare fish for local markets and canneries.

Above is the well-kept establishment of W. Barnes,
a purveyor of oysters near New Haven.
At left, a group of men inspects an impressive array
of fish flakes curing in the sun.

Overleaf: carts, wagons and drays crowd Boston's bustling Fish Pier.

Three Maine woodsmen show their tools of the trade: a crosscut saw,
a single-bladed poleaxe, and a double-bitted axe—one blade for chopping
and the other for trimming tree branches.

Above, cook's helpers use shoulder yokes to carry a substantial lunch out to the working woodsmen. There were two lunch breaks, at 10:00 A.M. and 2:00 P.M. Below, a lumberjack measures two colleagues at a Maine camp.

The message in this camp kitchen is "Complain about the food, I dare you."

A polite game of checkers proves unusually diverting for this group of loggers.

Work continued even
in the dead of winter
at a Maine logging camp.

At left, Maine loggers attack a tree with alternating strokes.

Above, a log is jacked onto a sled.

Overleaf: after cutting, timber was dragged to the riverside
to await spring thaw and a float downstream.

Above, woodsmen drive logs along a Maine river and boom them together
for floating across lakes.

At right, more precarious work was required at Livermore Falls
on the Beebee River in New Hampshire.

Strings of logs are neatly set up for a trip downriver.

This sawmill at Blanchard was in the Maine woods, near its source.

At the Norcross-West quarry (above) in South Dorset,
Vermont, cranes lifted immense blocks of marble more than a hundred feet.
The stoneworkers opposite cut granite at Barre, Vermont.

This group of quarrymen was probably photographed in western Massachusetts.

Above, oxen draw marble into a shop for carving.

Many Italian immigrants worked in Barre.
At right, workmen show the Corinthian capitals they have cut.

Two flatcars bear an immense granite obelisk
through snowy fields near Barre.

# III.

# IN THE TOWNS

Before the blight virtually wiped out the American elm,
nearly every New England town had its Elm Street.
Above is the one in Harrison, Maine, near Sebago Lake.

On the preceding page, in a picture dating from 1859,
the stately, columned Eagle Hotel overlooks the green
at Woodstock, Vermont.

I can stand in my door and hear a half dozen pianos, but I see but one acre of rye," a resident of the country town of Woodbury in Litchfield County, western Connecticut, wrote with some dismay in 1900. His town still had many acres on which rye was grown; it had an Agricultural Improvement Society and a noisy threshing mill where the grain was pounded. But it also had a population of around two thousand, and it had fire hydrants, and the old log horse-watering trough on Main Street had recently been replaced by one of granite. There were a barbershop and a drugstore, a resident doctor and a dentist—and an undertaker who traveled by bicycle to visit the family of the deceased and sold beds and furniture for the living as well as coffins for the dead. There was also a new golf links in town, built on what had once been farmland. Farmers didn't have time to play golf, but some townsfolk did.

Woodbury was one of scores of New England towns that had made the transition from being largely rural in character. Now it had become a small center of business and culture. It was not by any means urban; Waterbury, a few miles to the east, was the city of the region, with acres of factories and tenements and thousands of immigrants. Farther west were towns that were still almost completely rural. Woodbury was somewhere in between, and it prospered as a business center for outlying rural towns. Here were not one but two professional photographers before whom farmers and townsfolk posed for formal portraits. There was a jewelry store selling silverware made in Meriden, Connecticut, and clocks from Thomaston, Connecticut. There were two different stores that sold wallpaper. People could actually shop around. And as in many towns throughout New England, there was a new high school where the children of the town's rising middle class, the golfing crowd, could prepare for college. As in farming towns, the church—or rather the churches, for there were several—remained the focus of most social activity. But other organizations now competed with the church for the townspeople's time and money.

In the years after the Civil War, towns throughout New England were changing. Factories came to dominate some, increasing their population and permanently altering their character. Others lost their factories and became solidly residential; it was almost as if history had imposed zoning on them. Still others suddenly found themselves hosts to newly established colleges and became crowded with hundreds of alien and often incomprehensible youngsters. In the Berkshires and on the North Shore of Massachusetts, in Maine and New Hampshire, many towns became summer resorts. Others, particularly those near Boston and Providence, were suburbanized.

New residents arrived, destroying the rural character of the town. Often they formed organizations such as the Rural Improvement Company of Barrington in Rhode Island, whose aim was to deny the fact of suburbanization and maintain the fiction that the town was still a rural paradise.

By the end of the nineteenth century many of the towns were connected by miles of gleaming trolley tracks. In Connecticut and Rhode Island, the New York, New Haven, and Hartford Railroad ran trolleys along more than a thousand miles of track. Trolleys linked all the towns of the Merrimack Valley in Massachusetts and went over the border to Portsmouth in New Hampshire. In the Berkshires people could start out in Great Barrington in the southwest corner of Massachusetts and travel by trolley up to Bennington, Vermont, and then, if so minded, over into New York State. Trolleys connected almost all the suburbs of Boston and ran between Worcester and Springfield. Before the trolleys were electrified, there were horse railway companies which made trips on runners during the wintertime. "Good is this slender tie," a local poet wrote when the telegraph was introduced to join Woodbury, Connecticut, with the outside world. "Better iron bars. Thanks for the telegraph, but hurry up the cars." But no trolley line ever reached Woodbury.

Most people wanted to remain in their own towns, if they could, for there was immense local pride. Paradoxically, the trolley, which facilitated their leaving town, increased their chances of staying since it also made it easier for them to earn a living: men could commute to work in a nearby town, and outsiders could come into town to patronize local businesses. But even without the trolley, towns seemed to have many ties with the outside world. Some of the ties were literary. Rudyard Kipling came to live in one Vermont town; Sarah Orne Jewett added glory to another in Maine. Here, other townsfolk boasted, William Cullen Bryant had practiced law; here Daniel Webster had taught school. History was all around. Here, townsfolk could claim, Paul Revere rode by and here great-grandfather had carried the Marquis de Lafayette across a brook. No town was an island. Even insular towns—Nantucket with its whalers, Bar Harbor with its summer people, Vinalhaven with its Scandinavian quarrymen—were remarkably sophisticated.

But the outside world wasn't necessary; there was so much to do in town anyway. Men could join one of the town's many Masonic groups or the Knights of Pythias or the ancient Order of Foresters or the Improved Order of Red Men or the United Order of American Mechanics, all of which had their own meeting halls and meeting times and excitingly secret rules and rituals. (The Order of Red Men exchanged signs, grips, and passwords "drawn from the true culture of the American aborigines," seemingly impervious to the fact that the aborigines themselves were being subjected to genocide out West the way they once had been in New England.) Audubon societies met monthly to read and chat about birds. For those who were good at singing there were numerous church choirs, and for those who were good at listening there were frequent concerts to attend.

The ladies had their own groups, separate but equal. As early as 1805, Boston women had clubbed together to read books "favorable to the mind" and to deliver talks to each other on such subjects as "With How Much Religion Ought a Person Be Satisfied" and "The Disadvantages From Reading Novels." By the end of the nineteenth century, almost every town had similar women's clubs. Members wrote reports on local and world history and on books, and on such current issues as women's suffrage, and met to exchange ideas and "plan for progress." The women formed committees devoted to helping town charities, to building up the town library, to improving the town's musical life, and of course to arranging social gatherings. They held fairs to raise money for Sunday Schools, for famine sufferers abroad, and for the aged and infirm right in town. They cooked food for parties and collected "purses," i.e., cash gifts of several hundred dollars to celebrate the anniversaries of their ministers' twenty or twenty-five years of underpaid toil.

Townspeople labored most assiduously in the cause of temperance, to convince their fellow citizens of the evils of drink. Members of the Protestant Women's Christian Temperance Union and the Catholic Father Matthew Temperance Society opened reading rooms where actual or potential topers could read about the virtues of total abstinence. They gave regular lectures to the public on the perils of the saloons, and the W.C.T.U. raised money to buy up local barrooms and close them down. Women urged their husbands, often successfully, to vote to make the town dry, prohibiting all saloons and liquor sales, and they proselytized the young to enlist them for the cause. "Who was more manly than Samson, the world's strongest man?" boys who joined the Youth Temperance Society were asked. And Samson never touched a drop. Impressionable young boys, caught at the age of eight or nine, when high-minded sentiments are strong, signed the pledge and promised never to drink intoxicating beverages; many of them lived up to that promise for a lifetime. After all, any town boy knew that people could have lots of fun without drinking. There was fun all around—riding the trolleys, if the town had trolleys, or riding the express coach, if the town still relied on horsepower. There was building snow forts in the winter; and in the summer, there was the sport of teasing the older boys and girls who gathered nightly to sing songs in the new town park. Above all, there were the parades.

On Memorial Day, members of the local post of the Grand Army of the Republic held their annual meeting at a church or assembly hall and then marched solemnly to the graveyard to lay wreaths on the graves of their dead comrades. Another less solemn march led to the Soldiers' Monument, where the annual ceremonies were held: the ladies of the town presented a flag; ministers made speeches; the hymn "America" was sung; the new flag was raised; the crowd enthusiastically shouted out three rousing cheers for it; and soon it would be the Fourth of July.

Long before the Fourth, committees were formed to plan the parade and the program. There was an Executive Committee, a Parade Committee, a Reception Committee, and a Music Committee. Everybody got the chance to feel important — everybody, that is, who had acquired the leisure time in which to feel important. The town's surviving farmers had to remain content being important primarily to their cows, and the town's millhands were important mostly to the machines they operated. But they would show up to attend the parade anyway. Without their help the committees got together and worked hard to arrange an outstanding program. At sunrise on the Fourth there was a gun salute from a prominent hill overlooking town. Then there was, as one parade report describes it, a "merry chime" from all of the town's churches — the Congregationalist (familiarly known as the Congo), the Methodist, the Episcopalian, the Catholic, and the Baptist. (Rhode Island had a bouquet of Baptist churches: ordinary Baptists and Freewill Baptists and Six-Principle Baptists and Seventh Day Baptists, and, in some towns, the First Baptist Church, Colored.) Meanwhile householders, particularly those on Main Street along which the parade would pass, would have "tastefully" adorned their houses with flags, and all the public buildings had been decked out with bunting. Often the drum corps of a neighboring town was imported for the march. As the parade got underway, the dignitaries who would be orating to the townsfolk about patriotism and glory rode by in carriages; behind them, in another carriage, appeared the town centenarian and those citizens in their nineties whose parents or grandparents had been around to celebrate the Fourth of July in 1776. Parade floats depicted "Freedom Defended by the Army and the Navy" and the "Thirteen Original Colonies," while other floats just as ornate represented the local feed dealer and the boot and shoe store. In towns without trolleys, the express coach that transported people to the nearest train station would take its place in the line of march, and out of the barns would come old-fashioned coaches driven by people wearing old-fashioned costumes. There was a band concert, there were speeches, there were poetry recitations, there were prayers, there were choir selections, there was the singing of "America," and as soon as it got dark, there were fireworks. A wonderful time was had by all.

Every town had occasions for civic celebration. A new town hall or a new high school was built; the trolley line finally came through; a new business block was opened; or the electric lights were turned on. Throughout New England, as throughout America, the post–Civil War era was an age of expansion. New free public libraries by the score were opened throughout the region, with rich benefactors endowing towns with fine library buildings—imitation Romanesque castles made of fireproof cut stone and designed by leading architects. New town halls reflected the towns' consciousness of their changing status, and new high schools reflected the obsolescence of the one-room schoolhouse. There were frequent sober, high-minded celebrations as town after town dedicated its own Temperance Hall.

Along the broad streets of the towns, big, roomy new houses went up by the thousands. Some had mansard roofs in the latest French-inspired style; some were expanded versions of old New England farmhouses with pitched roofs and green or black shutters; some were romantic wooden versions of English gentlemen's houses with turrets and balconies and stained-glass windows and roofs of Vermont slate. And some were in a new, locally developed style, today called the Stick Style, with fancy brackets and pickets under the roofline, and with porches upstairs and down. Actually almost all of the houses had porches, great sweeping expanses where little girls played with their dolls on rainy days. Indoors there were tile fireplaces, ornamental rather than merely useful. For the advent of steam heat had made life more comfortable, and fireplaces weren't really necessary. The silence of snowy winter streets was broken by the creak of the coal dealer's wagon and the rattle of coal running down the chute into cellar coal bins. It became the town boy's job to shake down the ashes from the furnace grate each morning, as it had always been the farm boy's job to fill the woodbox.

There were other modern improvements, with electric light in every room the greatest marvel of them all. After the Civil War, bathtubs with running water became common. A new invention called the lawn mower made its appearance, and now people could have expansive, closely cropped lawns beneath their apple and maple trees. In the kitchens there were enormous up-to-date coal-burning cast-iron stoves and attached to them—wonder of wonders!—were water heaters. Now above her soapstone sink, a housewife could have access to hot as well as cold water, making it much easier for her and her daughter to do the dishes.

Dishes of course were always woman's work. There was no flexibility about sex roles in these houses, although the housewife, after finishing her dishes, might go out to the new public library and read about the exciting advances being made in the status of women. In 1881, for example, Massachusetts passed a law actually giving some property rights to married women: they now legally owned their own clothing.

To accommodate these houses and the growing populations of the towns, new streets were laid out over what had recently been farmland. Developers and town fathers stretched their imaginations to name them. Usually their imaginations weren't stretched very far, and town after town across New England constructed Linden and Locust streets and Elmwood and Woodside avenues. Hero streets—Farraguts and Garfields and Deweys—by the dozen stretched across the landscape, and many towns built Amherst, Harvard, Dartmouth, and Bowdoin streets. In one Massachusetts seaside town, streets were, more fancifully, named Trident, Neptune, Sea Foam, Coral, Dolphin, and Pearl; but such flights were the exception.

"Hen-roost robbers have begun their annual depredations," the Northampton, Massachusetts, newspaper reported in 1879. "A couple of fellows with a buggy and a light-colored horse called at a house on Maple Street Saturday night and while one of them visited a hen-roost, the other with the team waited just around the corner." As the towns grew in size, they gained sophistication but they also lost much of their innocence. Everyone no longer belonged to the same church and had the same values. Class distinctions became more important. Business and professional people lived in one world and millworkers in another; so did Protestants and Catholics and the various ethnic groups who began to move in. By the end of the nineteenth century towns had become so sophisticated that some people customarily locked the doors of their houses.

Leyden Street, in Plymouth, Massachusetts, purports to be New England's oldest street.

Above, a Deerfield, Massachusetts gentleman
strolls the tree-lined main street.

At right, a squad of leaf rakers tidies up Newfields, New Hampshire.

Quiet town pasttimes:
at left, the Hobbs family, harness makers of Wenham, Massachusetts,
poses for a group portrait including their house and shop;
below, a Lincoln, Rhode Island trio relaxes.

A Farmington, Connecticut father and a homegrown quartet make music.

A Massachusetts dining room is set for
Halloween dinner.

On December 26, 1907,
this Londonderry, Vermont baby
was photographed beside
the Christmas tree.

A back porch railing in Wenham, Massachusetts serves as a frame for a hooked rug.

On days off, the hammocks in Sanford, Maine backyards got a good workout.

Like most town kids, Norfolk, Connecticut children enjoyed an occasional hayride.

The baseball bats wait while
these western Massachusetts youngsters have their picture taken.

Rhode Island birthday parties, then as now, featured a standard but wonderful menu.

Norfolk girls take their sewing seriously.

The handsome brick school in Hadley, Massachusetts
stood decked in bunting in 1909 to celebrate the town's 250th anniversary.

Under teacher's watchful eye, Avon, Connecticut schoolchildren read a Fourth of July story.

On the following pages, business is conducted
in a bustling Bennington, Vermont grocery store.

In Massachusetts, fresh bread and cakes came door to door.

A Sanford, Maine butcher shows the latest in delivery wagons, and incidentally, his young son.

In summer, business went out-of-doors in Putney, Vermont.

The Horn of Plenty ice cream parlor in Osterville kept Cape Cod tourists well refreshed.

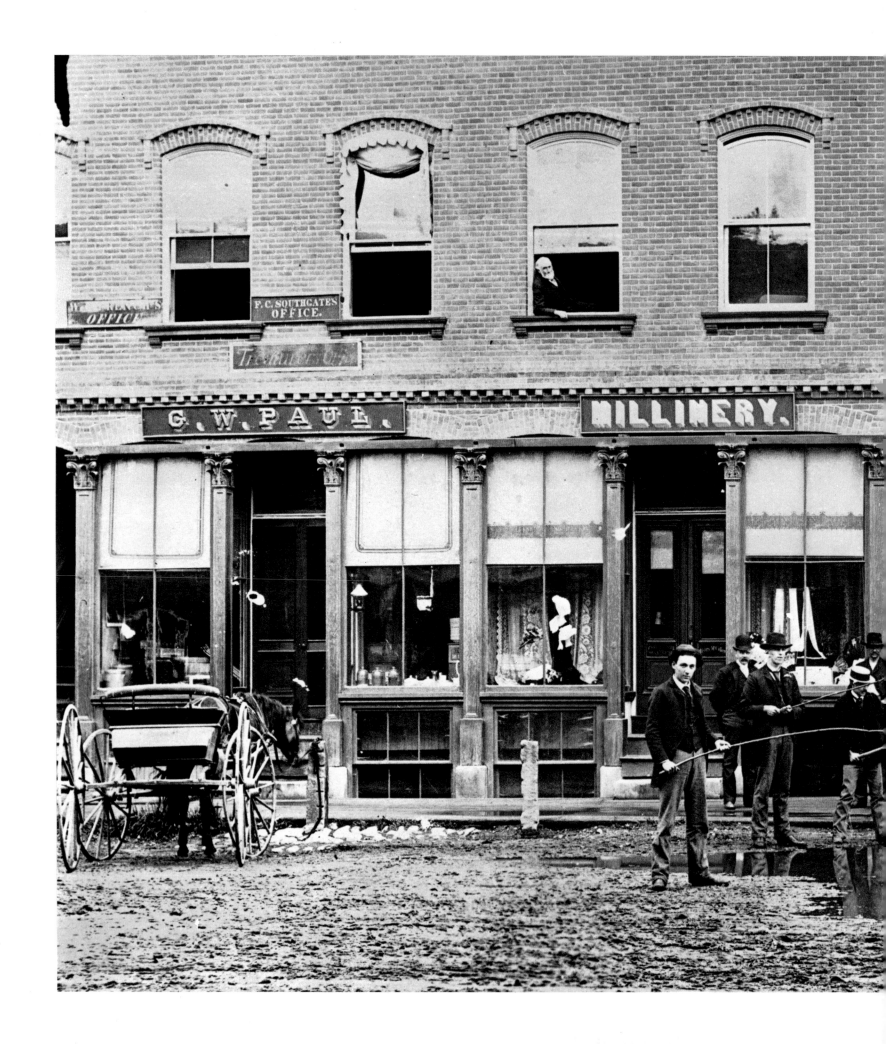

Before Woodstock, Vermont's main street was paved, village wags pretended to fish in a spring mud puddle outside the post office.

Above, a dissident tennis player gets in on the act of the Bicycle Club of Limerick, Maine.

At left, members of the Sanford, Maine Canoe Club prepare for an outing on the Mousam River.

On the following pages, members of a Norfolk, Connecticut gymnasium
demonstrate that physical fitness is serious business.

The town band of Cherryfield, Maine sported splendid uniforms.

In Essex, Vermont (right), a musical group played for a minstrel show.

Above, the townsfolk of Plainfield, Connecticut turn out to see the touring Liberty Bell.

At left, above, children in Canterbury, New Hampshire, carry flowers
to decorate graves on Memorial Day.

At left, below, in time-honored tradition, a Fourth of July speaker holds forth
at Arlington, Vermont.

250th ANNIVERSARY
JUNE, 5, 6, 7th
1904
NORTHAMPTON MASS.

At Northampton, Massachusetts'
250th anniversary celebration in 1904, the float at left,
made by the townspeople of German descent,
portrays 2,000 years of Teutonic history.

Seven years later, another group of Northamptonites (above)
got themselves up as Pilgrims for a pageant.

Fourth of July parades were often a town's biggest social event.
Above, the schoolchildren of Middleborough, Massachusetts, play their part.

A festive flotilla of horse-drawn carriages crowds the flag-draped main street
of Winthrop, Maine.

Dressed in their best, townsfolk and summer people turn out for an open-air

entertainment in the Connecticut River town of Walpole, New Hampshire.

# IV.

# SUMMER PEOPLE

Cape Cod beach cottagers lunch *al fresco*, with watermelon for dessert.

On the preceding page, a Connecticut sand monster fooled no one,
but was worth a snapshot.

**M**rs. Stylington Ribblehurst, a stalwart of New York society, came to Bar Harbor and so did that famous New York swell, Poodle Van Ulster, and the equally famous New York belle, Lina Van Rooster, reported an 1890 guidebook to the Maine resort, gently spoofing the rich who had taken over a fishing village and turned it into a splendid summer resort in an age when high society was really high. The lineage of the New York visitors was no more ancient than that of the locals who sold them their groceries in Maine; in fact, some of the natives traced their land titles back to a feudal grant from the king of France, whose representatives arrived in Bar Harbor before the Vanderbilts did. But the New Yorkers had the money and the natives didn't, and by the end of the nineteenth century Bar Harbor had turned into a summer colony of New York. As a result of the summer people's arrival, Bar Harbor even changed its name. Originally, it had been the town of Eden, a perfect name for a vacation place; Bar Harbor was just one section of town, where the fashionable people built their expensive cottages. But in the hope of luring more free-spending visitors and spreading their money around, the golden name became legally fixed to the entire town.

Bar Harbor was only one of many New England coast and mountain towns that were taken over permanently by summer people. Most retained their original names, but all lost their original character. Not all the summer people came from New York, of course, although it was New Yorkers who made the most spectacular impression, as they escaped the city to spend their summers close to nature, where they could talk about stock prices as they strolled through formal gardens and dance until dawn in casinos, with windows open to let in the sea air. Rich Philadelphians bought acres of land in Maine overlooking Penobscot Bay, north of Camden, and many towns became the resort of rich and middle-class New Englanders. Some even became miniature Coney Islands for local factory workers.

Along the Maine coast, New Yorkers left the island of Manhattan to colonize, not only Bar Harbor on Mount Desert Island but also Dark Harbor at Islesboro; and some, including one aristocratic family named Roosevelt, went all the way down the coast to Campobello Island, over the line in New Brunswick. New Yorkers turned Greenwich and the nearby Connecticut towns into a rich man's ghetto. At first the Connecticut shore towns were summer resorts; then they became year-round retreats. New Yorkers made Newport a synonym for the life of the idle and ostentatious rich; those who couldn't afford to be quite so ostentatious as the Newport rich, but still yearned for the Rhode Island shore, contented themselves with spending their summers at Narragansett Pier. At Newport, most visitors stayed the entire season until the end of August; then they retired to Lenox or Stockbridge in the Berkshires of

Massachusetts, and there they remained throughout the autumn and sometimes even as late as November, when the foliage had fallen in New England and the tempo of the parties had risen in New York.

Life in these resorts was heavenly for what one 1886 description of Newport called "that large and growing class of people who live for enjoyment and possess sufficient wealth to gratify their desires." Members of that class of people lived in "palatial villas, surrounded by beautiful grounds, where wealth and art have accomplished all that the highest culture and the most lavish expenditure could achieve." Although it did not have fox hunting like Lenox, Newport had a horse show and championship tennis matches and a daily 9:00 A.M. dress parade at the naval station and an 11:00 A.M. concert at the Casino for those who didn't care to swim during the fashionable bathing hour, which was from 11:00 A.M. to 12:00 noon. It even had a colony of notable intellectuals—the writer Henry James and his brother William, the philosopher and Harvard professor; the painter John La Farge; the eminent poet and reformer Julia Ward Howe, who had written "The Battle Hymn of the Republic." But these worthies weren't of much interest to people who lived for enjoyment. The New Yorkers didn't enjoy abstract pleasures, only concrete ones; and for their pleasures enormously rich Astors, Goelets, Belmonts, and Vanderbilts constructed vast shingled cottages with lots of rooms in the attic for the servants, or imitation French châteaux and Italian palazzi with three-story center halls adorned with frescoes, friezes, and fretwork. These mansions had music rooms and billiard rooms and ballrooms and drawing rooms and morning rooms and breakfast rooms and state dining rooms. They were more than adequately comfy.

But there was another, simpler New England vacation life whose devotees disdained soft living and went in for energetic swimming in the sea or across the lake, brisk walks and mountain climbs, canoeing, sailing, and fishing. Summer boarders began going to the White Mountains before the Civil War, and by 1857 Thoreau had made three excursions to the woods of northern Maine, taking a steamer up to Bangor from Boston and then paddling upriver with an Indian guide. Bar Harbor's popularity began, as had that of so many resorts, when artists, who were attracted by the scenery, came to work there during the summer; they lived simply, boarding with the natives. Thomas Cole and Albert Bierstadt and men of their ilk came first. J.P. Morgan and men of his ilk followed.

Throughout northern New England were farms that took in summer people as boarders; eventually some farmers added an ell to the house to accommodate more visitors. Taking in guests was easier and more remunerative than farmwork. ("Bury the frying pan in the farmyard," farmwives who contemplated taking in summer boarders were advised; city people didn't like greasy food.) Many farmers expanded their farmhouses into hotels, and by 1875 travelers to the mountains or the coast could choose from many hotels. Most of them were small and primitive, but a few were as lavish as Newport's Ocean House with its gables and Gothic doorways and piazzas hundreds of feet long, where guests might sit and rock and watch to see whose carriage went by. Ocean View Houses and Mount Pleasant Houses and Ravine Houses and Grand View Hotels arose at scenic spots. At first hotel life was not very elaborate. Guests gathered in parlors, often no more than fourteen feet square, with home-woven carpets on the floor, big wood stoves in the corner, kerosene lamps hanging from the ceiling, and some not very comfortable chairs on which to sit. In the White Mountains the visitors were usually quite sophisticated Bostonians. One might be a Harvard professor marking out trails through the mountains and another a bookseller, who entertained the other guests with anecdotes of Emerson and Longfellow.

Tourists rode over mountain roads in horse-drawn buckboards driven by local farmers or went fishing or canoeing or walked along mountain paths; by the turn of the century miles of trails had been blazed for them in the White Mountains by the Appalachian Mountain Club. Still, a Baedeker guidebook warned: "A good pocket compass is necessary, especially in the woods." The more adventurous could climb to the top of Mount Washington to see Arctic flora without having to go all the way to the Arctic. But as early as 1869, there were so many tourists in the White Mountains that people didn't have to make the climb by foot anymore if they didn't want to; a cog railway was built to take them to the top, and soon the summit was being visited by about ten thousand tourists each year.

A small industry arose providing guidebooks for summer visitors. It was an age that hungered for the picturesque, and post–Civil War magazines were filled with stories set in old Marblehead or old Cape Cod, or along the coast of Maine. Rockport, Massachusetts, is much "haunted" by artists, one guidebook informed thrill-seeking tourists. Newport is "the undisputed Queen of American Seaside Resorts," said another. Provincetown, like many other places, was "a quaint old fishing town," and on the North Shore of Massachusetts, Swampscott was "charming" and Winthrop was a town of "delightful peacefulness and decorum." Some summer places had "pure sea air and immunity from mosquitoes"; others were havens for hay-fever sufferers. Some lake resorts in Maine were "sporting centers" and others were "fine sporting centers." The finer sporting centers were pretty far up-country, for by the 1870s salmon, which had once been so abundant, was gone from all the rivers south and west of the Kennebec. Those resorts that were deepest in the woods were "a veritable sportsman's paradise," where lake trout and landlocked salmon could be found, along with moose, deer, and other game. But even in paradise there were game laws; by the 1880s there were official salmon seasons and moose seasons in the state of Maine.

Resorts tried to live up to the promises of the guidebooks and embellish the picturesqueness with which nature had endowed them. When the Romantic artist Frederic Church saw an eagle flying over Great Pond at Bar Harbor, he immediately rechristened the pond Eagle Lake. Eagle Lakes tend to attract more tourists than Great Ponds do, and canny natives everywhere quickly caught on to the idea. Soon there was a Wizard's Glen and a Flora Glen in the Berkshires, and on the map of the White Mountains appeared an Artist's Falls, a Crystal Cascade, an Echo Lake, and a Devil's Den. The changes made everybody happy.

It wasn't only grownups who had to be made happy. Children went on vacation, too, away from the unhealthy air of the city and the usually inescapable presence of their parents. The first organized summer camp for boys was established in 1881 along the shores of Squam Lake in central New Hampshire's lake country. Soon there were others. In 1884 Worcester's Natural History Society opened a natural history camp at a lake outside the city. The boys in residence there got up at 6:00 A.M. at reveille and then began grappling energetically with a program of gymnastics, athletics, and intellectual and moral self-improvement. They learned how to pitch a tent, handle an ax, and row a boat. They were taught how to identify a bird, shoot it, stuff it, and mount it. There were bee hunts and lectures on "Success in Business" and on "The Mollusca of the Lake"; and before taps at 9:30 P.M. tales were told around the campfire about the Indians of the Worcester region. (The camp's tents were pitched at the foot of an eminence labeled Wigwam Hill.) Any boy too exhausted to stay awake until 9:30 was allowed to go to bed immediately after the dress parade at sunset. Within a few years, a summer camp for girls was started across the lake from the boys' camp so that girls might enjoy "some of the advantages which their brothers have." Some, but not all. Members of the weaker sex might be strong enough to get stung on a successful bee hunt, but they weren't strong enough to be lectured at on the necessity of succeeding in business.

And then there were the pious, whose modest vacation and uplift retreats appeared all over New England. Some of their settlements, like that at Winthrop on Massachusetts's North Shore, were merely mildly evangelical villages, "with every evening devoted to . . . musicales, square dancing or chapel-going." Others developed from Methodist camp-meeting grounds like Cottage City on Martha's Vineyard, where dozens of tiny gingerbread cottages were built around an open-air tabernacle. At Cottage City the faithful benefited from lusty hymn singing, invigorating sea air, and even more invigorating sermons. But other vacationers, whose values and interests were different from theirs, were attracted to the site and with their coming, Cottage City changed. A casino was built, and hotels, where alcoholic beverages were sold, opened up. Cottage City lost its good name and became Oak Bluffs.

Inevitably, there were complaints about the tourists—even about the pious ones. They drove up prices for the natives; they broke the game laws; they were litterbugs. "Every fair day," reported an 1874 magazine article on Peak Island, Maine, "the steamboat was crowded with excursion parties visiting the islands of Casco Bay, or carrying 'campers' who establish themselves in tents . . . for two or three weeks at a time and leave behind them in the pine groves at the close of the season a varied assortment of clam shells, empty bottles and broken crockery." The hoi polloi were coming.

Social gradations emerged among the vacationers, or summer people, as the hometown folks called them. At the bottom of the heap were the day-trippers who arrived by train, trolley, or excursion boat. Above them were the hotel guests who came for a week or two. But there were classy hotels and less classy hotels; and even within individual hotels, important social distinctions existed. "Frequent change of dress," one guidebook to the White Mountains warned around 1900, "has become all too usual at the larger hotels, but those whose object is rather outdoor exercise than indoor frivolity need not yield to this custom more than they choose." The frivolous scorned the outdoor exercisers, who in turn scorned the frivolous right back. Another, more unpleasant distinction began to appear as the nineteenth century came to a close and hotels began discriminating among their prospective guests: many hotels closed their doors to Jews. Not everybody approved. When William James received a hotel circular announcing that "applications from Hebrews cannot be considered," he sent back an answer announcing, "I propose to return the boycott."

At the top of the social pyramid were those who owned their own summer houses, whether they were cottages along the shore in middle-class vacation towns or imitation Versailles cottages at Newport (one of the most notable of which, by the way, belonged to Oliver H.P. Belmont, who happened to be the scion of a Hebrew family). In Newport, those fashionables who didn't own a cottage or wangle an invitation to one stayed at certain chic "boardinghouses" and never at hotels, for the Newport hotels weren't good enough for those who had already arrived in high society; they were suitable only for people who enjoyed watching high society from afar. And summer cottages much simpler than those of Newport certainly outranked hotels on Boston's North Shore. Along that coast, there were a few hotels, but their social quality can be judged by the fact that the most fashionable of them, the Masconomo at Magnolia, had begun as a resort run by people connected with the *theater*. The North Shore was better typified by Nahant, with its chilly ocean waters and its literary visitors such as Longfellow and Oliver Wendell Holmes, whose interests and conversation were quite different from those of the Vanderbilts and Mrs. Stylington Ribblehurst. In 1890 a Boston newspaper compared New England's two most august summer resorts: "The tendencies to more frivolous and more luxurious habits of life in New York are at Newport highly accentuated . . . while Nahant, on the other hand, maintains the pristine dignity and aristocratic quality which have given to Boston her fame among cities."

But even pristine Nahant had an amusement park where working people could enjoy themselves by the sea. For it wasn't only the rich who longed for what Longfellow, inspired by his summer retreat at Nahant, called "the sound of the trampling surf/On the rocks and the hard sea sand." Improvements in transportation had brought the New York rich to Bar Harbor and swarms of proper Bostonians to the North Shore and had opened Cape Cod, New Hampshire, and Maine to the middle class; by 1910 more than three hundred thousand vacationers came to New Hampshire annually. Now the electric trolleys made it possible for the city poor to get out of their tenements and on to the beach too. Amusement parks sprang up along the shores of New England. Many of them were built as investments by the trolley-car companies which laid down tracks leading to them so that the poor could take vacations by the day for the price of two fares, a nickel for going out to the beach and a nickel for coming home. In New Haven a trolley line extended out to a small amusement park at Lighthouse Point. New Bedford millhands traveled to Lincoln Park in nearby Dartmouth, and on the New Hampshire coast boisterous Hampton Beach attracted factory workers from the cities nearby. Rhode Islanders went to beaches along the shores of Narragansett Bay, and at Revere Beach near Boston arose an amusement park that almost rivaled Coney Island itself. Revere had two roller coasters, a roller-skating rink, boxing matches, and nightly fireworks to amuse visitors; it had band concerts, bowling alleys, shooting galleries, and a merry-go-round which Massachusetts people called "the flying horses." Newport and Bar Harbor couldn't boast of that. The workingman who spent fifty cents at Revere Beach on a day's excursion would probably be happier, one Boston newspaper advised, than "the man of wealth who makes a tour to Saratoga and wears himself and a $50 bill out." Immense crowds were attracted to the beach; in 1888, eight thousand members of the National Irish Association convened there. But they weren't the only ones who came. Pickpockets, confidence men, and drunks came too. Revere, as one observer wrote, "attracted a rough and disorderly element and nearly the whole shore was occupied by the cheapest kind of shanties, used for undesirable purposes."

Revere's visitors may not have been uniformly wonderful, but its beach was. The beach was two miles long, gently sloping and sandy, and the average summer temperature of its water was considerably warmer than the fifty-eight degrees the society people had to cope with in Nahant, which was always in sight a few miles away across the water. In 1893 Massachusetts took over Revere Beach and made it a public park, the first beach in America to be set aside for the residents of a major city. A broad boulevard and a public bathhouse were built and every shanty between the boulevard and the water was torn down, even if it hadn't been used for undesirable purposes. It was an age when the cities, packed with immigrants, were becoming too crowded, unhealthy, and uncomfortable. Now everybody, no matter how poor, could escape the treeless tenement streets and get close to nature. Unfortunately, at Revere Beach, just as at Newport and Bar Harbor, that often involved getting a little too close to human nature as well.

New Hampshire's Mount Washington Hotel, with accommodations for five hundred guests
at a pricey five to six dollars a day, was "a great resort of automobilists,"
as a turn-of-the-century guidebook reported.

A stained-glass windowed rotunda, gleaming columns, and an ample supply of wicker chairs
and potted palms made the Mount Washington Hotel the most elegant resort
in the White Mountains.

Risking their dignity, a good-natured quartet of rusticators
mounts up for a trail ride.

At right, a few of the 15,000 summer visitors who yearly flocked
to Bethlehem, New Hampshire relax on a hotel porch.

On the following pages, in a gala end-of-season parade
at North Conway, New Hampshire, the Casco Bay Steamboat Company
of Portland, Maine entered a jaunty float.

Smaller vacation hotels and cottage camps flourished
among the giant resorts of New England's mountains and shore.

Above, a heated croquet match engages the guests at The Highland
in Bethlehem, New Hampshire.

Opposite, a family relaxes at Camp Idlewild in North Hero, Vermont.

New England's myriad lakes offered summer refreshment for thousands of city dwellers:
New Hampshire youths learned to swim and dive at Pine Island pond in Manchester.

A family proves that the fishing was pretty good in 1898
on Sebasticook Lake in Newport, Maine.

A swimming party poses at Lake Dunmore near Middlebury, Vermont.

The Vermont hunters at left came to the woods well equipped.
Above, at Rangeley Lakes, Maine, a dockside discussion
near a pair of elegant lapstrake canoes engages two vacationers.

Crafts, sports, fresh air, and wholesome food made city kids
perk up at camps throughout New England.
Overleaf: in the left hand column are scenes at Camp Wyonegonic in Maine;
at right is New Hampshire's Camp Kehonka.

Notable for its pure mineral water, Poland Spring,
Maine, saw its first inn open in 1797.
By 1906, Poland Spring House had a front lawn big enough for golf.

Ferries all along the New England coast carried vacationers and daytrippers
to hundreds of island beaches.

Above, the streamlined sidewheeler Bay Queen, built in 1865, boards passengers for
Narragansett Bay resorts.

Above, an eccentric group of Newport,
Rhode Islanders had the beach all to themselves.

At left, Grandpa, Fido, and the girls
explore a wreck at Nantucket.

Beach picnic fare in Maine naturally ran to lobster and clams.
Above, the ladies take charge of the fixings.

Near a fisherman's shack at Popham Beach, the stand-up treats included corn fritters and sarsaparilla.

Even the rather tepid waters of
Long Island Sound delighted bathers at Madison, Connecticut.

At left, a sailing party evokes mixed reactions near
Appledore Island, Maine.

The millhands of Lawrence and Lowell
contented themselves with a Sunday lark at the amusement park
in Salisbury Beach, Massachusetts (above).

Well-to-do New Yorkers, many of whom stayed the whole season, relax on
the patio of the Casino (right) at Narragansett Pier, Rhode Island.

At New Haven, the strand and pier on Sundays were very nearly as crowded as the city streets.

# V.

# IN THE MILLS

Above, Brockton, Massachusetts cobblers assemble shoes.

On the preceding page, the mills at Lowell, Massachusetts
were conveniently situated near their power source,
the Merrimack River.

The fastest express train in the world wouldn't be swift enough to carry off all the cloth woven daily in the great Massachusetts cotton center of Fall River, that city's businessmen boasted. About 1900 Fall River produced fifteen hundred miles of cotton cloth a day, and no train could travel that distance in twenty-four hours. Like modern Texans, nineteenth-century New Englanders liked to brag, in numbers, and they had a lot to brag about. Throughout the century New England produced wealth so plentifully that it was the industrial heart of America. With ample waterpower and a density of population unequaled anywhere in the United States, New England had inaugurated America's industrial revolution. But as the century progressed, other regions became industrialized, and by the 1880s the nation's leading manufacturing center was not a New England town; it was Pittsburgh. Still the country's second manufacturing town was Lowell and its third was Fall River. Textiles, in which New England specialized, were America's second most important industry.

New England schoolchildren learned that the Merrimack turned more spindles than any other river in the world; that Boston was the world's leading shoe and leather center; that New England had the largest mill building in the world, the Wood Mill in Lawrence, which was a third of a mile long. Actually that mill, with its fifty-five hundred millhands, wasn't even Lawrence's largest employer. Another mill paid off sixty-five hundred hands every Saturday afternoon and yet another paid off seven thousand. New England had the largest cotton manufacturer in the world, the Amoskeag Manufacturing Company in Manchester, New Hampshire, with seventeen thousand workers; there were generations of them, grandparents, parents, and children, all at work in the same mill. Amoskeag had its own hydroelectric power station and printing plant, its own canals and railroad tracks, its own boardinghouses and tenements where the company's workers lived. In immense rooms, lit by immense windows, immense looms clattered ceaselessly in dozens of buildings set behind spiky, wrought-iron gates that could close permanently against a worker rash enough to disobey his foreman.

There were hundreds of smaller factories in hundreds of towns throughout the six states. Almost every town of any size had one. All together they produced an enormous variety of goods. Ninety percent of the horsewhips made in America, in the days when buggy whips were big business, were manufactured in Westfield, Massachusetts; and a few miles to the east, in Springfield, the first American automobile was manufactured—the machine that would make the buggy whip obsolete. Most of the world's fine mechanic's tools came from the Massachusetts town of Athol. St. Johnsbury in Vermont was famous for scales. Books were manufactured in

Cambridge, Massachusetts, and Holyoke was the greatest paper center in the world. Hats were made in Norwalk and Danbury, Connecticut; and Fall River produced five thousand derbies a day, using three million rabbit skins a year to do it. Waltham, Massachusetts, produced a million watches a year; Waterbury, Connecticut, six hundred thousand. In Brattleboro, Vermont, twenty thousand church and parlor organs were manufactured yearly. In Massachusetts, Gardner produced four million chairs a year, and one factory's machines in Rhode Island spewed out almost three million metal files and rasps annually.

The power for all this industry was traditionally provided by waterwheels—there were ten thousand of them in 1908 running the turbines that ran the machines. More power came from the steam engine, which allowed many seaside towns without waterpower to develop industry anyway since they could import coal cheaply by water. Smokestacks rose over the landscape; one in Cambridge, it was proudly pointed out, was higher than the Bunker Hill Monument. And New England added power to power. A water turbine, invented by a Holyoke mechanic, increased the power produced by the traditional overshot waterwheel by almost a third. Another New England invention, the Corliss steam engine, developed and manufactured in Providence, was a major technological advance. "No invention since Watt's time has so enhanced the efficiency of the steam engine," proclaimed the Academy of Arts and Sciences in Boston when it awarded a medal to its inventor, George H. Corliss.

In town after town, soon after the factory whistle blew at 6:00 A.M. to awaken the workers, the turbines, steam- or water-driven, started the machines going. Most of their power was used to produce textiles, for the typical New England millhand worked in a textile mill. In the textile towns, which might be as large as Lawrence or as small as the mill towns that dotted the river valleys of Rhode Island, a worker's day started as soon as the factory whistle blew. Inside the mill, the workers climbed the stairs to the weaving or carding rooms; there they stood for twelve hours tending their machines in the noise, dust, and lint, replacing bobbins, carrying them from the bobbin winder to the loom and then back again, or feeding wool or cotton to the carding machines; as a result of the dust, many of them suffered from respiratory diseases. In the enormous city mills hundreds worked in each room, many of them inhabitants of the company's tenement houses, if they were married, or its boardinghouses if they were not. Some were Yankee, some Irish, and some French, although the French often weren't around in the summer since they tended to leave for Quebec to help on the family farm; they returned at the beginning of September, after the early Canadian harvest. After the 1890s, many were Italian or Greek or Polish or Portuguese, and always a great many of them were women. But eventually fewer and fewer women worked in the mills; immigrant boys were stronger and just as cheap. From 1870 on the percentage of women in the textile work force declined, although it never got very low.

Workers had to be on hand early to put in their twelve hours a day, until pressure from unions and reformers decreased the number of working hours. In 1887 the Maine legislature cut work hours for women and children under sixteen from sixty-six to sixty hours a week; by 1911 in Massachusetts and by 1916 in Maine the workweek was down to fifty-four hours. Early in the nineteenth century, the millhands' twelve-hour day had been relatively leisurely; the pace was slow and workers had time to chat, tell stories, and play games while tending their machines. But after the Civil War there was a speedup in the big cotton mills. Each millgirl was given more looms to tend, and even the machines were made to move faster. It was becoming increasingly clear that time is money. By the end of the nineteenth century when most of the work force was made up of immigrants, conditions in the mills were often harrowing. "It was as though you were in jail," reported one Amoskeag worker who spent his days winding spinning frames.

In all the mills, filled with lint and lit by kerosene lamps until electricity became common, fire was a constant danger and workers couldn't smoke, though they could take snuff. There were disastrous fires, and carelessly built mills collapsed, killing hundreds. Eventually, late in the nineteenth century, insurance companies provided plans for building solid, fireproof mill buildings. As a result of their designs, which so many textile companies wisely followed in constructing new mill buildings, mills came to seem interchangeable. Workers were interchangeable too, except for those with special skills. And the immigrant groups were also interchangeable. The Irish replaced the Yankees; the French replaced the Irish; and the southern and Eastern Europeans replaced the French—with Greeks in Lowell and Manchester, Portuguese in southeastern New England, and Poles in the Connecticut Valley. The textile mills frequently advertised for help in Europe, for new immigrants would work harder and more cheaply than Americans, and when immigrant ships arrived in Boston, factory representatives were on the wharves ready to offer jobs to the new arrivals who had been enticed here by their advertisements.

Certain groups weren't interchangeable though. These were the skilled laborers, often English immigrants, who worked as loom fixers and mule spinners and weavers, and when they went out on strike, they couldn't easily be replaced by unskilled operatives right off the boat. They formed powerful unions soon after the Civil War. It wasn't until the 1890s that ordinary workers had unions and dared go out on strike with some hope of success. But very often success eluded them. When textile workers went out on strike in one Maine mill in 1900, management grandly offered to take back to work "with no discrimination on political, religious or social connections" anyone who would stop striking. The suspect political connection might be Socialist; the suspect religious connection was Roman Catholic; and the suspect social connection was union membership. When the strike continued despite the offer, all the workers were fired. That ended the strike. Everywhere management fought vigorously and harshly against recognizing unions, and everywhere it cut back wages when times were hard. In 1898 wage cutbacks led to a wave of strikes which spread throughout New England, making it difficult for millowners to import strikebreakers from other towns to man the machines as was customary.

If orders slowed down, millhands were generally laid off. If they were in a small town they had the option of going back to the farm or out to the clamflats to dig for food or maybe to travel into Boston or another city to look for work. If they lived in a town like Boston, Providence, or Bridgeport, which had varied industries, they were better off. In Bridgeport, if things were slow at the sewing machine plant, work might be found in the ammunition factories or in the winter quarters of Barnum and Bailey's Circus; or workers could travel into New Haven or Norwalk or to the mill towns of the Naugatuck Valley in search of work. But in a one-company town like Amoskeag's Manchester, hard times were inescapable if they came; and if you were so unfortunate as to get your name on a company's blacklist, you couldn't be hired anywhere.

The decades before and after the turn of the century were a time of great labor unrest. The factory system, which had seemed to be bringing so much good when it first appeared in New England at the beginning of the nineteenth century, didn't seem quite so appealing anymore and it was being reexamined. In company towns, millowners tried to promote the idea that the company was just one big happy family; but the millhands themselves often thought that was a joke, and not a very good one at that. They weren't happy about the fact that their own families usually had no place to go except into the mill, generation after generation, or into another mill in an identical mill town. Strikes, such as that of the Lowell mule spinners in 1867 and 1875, were often counterproductive; they inspired technological improvements which helped make the striking workers unnecessary. In the 1870s and 1880s new technology rendered hundreds of small, hand-operated shoe shops in Lynn and Brockton obsolete, and shoeworkers were replaced by machines. Millhands, thrown out of work, usually had no place to go for help. In 1894 thousands of them marched on the Massachusetts statehouse demanding jobs. Of course there were no jobs there. The government wasn't a big employer then and couldn't do anything for them, and the workers were soon dispersed. In town after town imposing brick National and State

Guard armories were built, partly because the Guard might have to be called out to put down strikers, as it was in Lawrence during the bitter 1912 textile strike. Strikers were mostly foreign-born anyway, "the off-scourings of south Europe," as one guardsman who served in Lawrence wrote.

In response to these unpleasant conditions, new ideas began circulating. In the 1880s, at Harvard, a hero of the abolition movement, Wendell Phillips, shocked his audience when he proposed that the university join with the workers to battle corporations. Phillips called for the "overthrow of the whole profit-making system." In Boston the United Labor Party ran a candidate for mayor. In 1894 the First Labor Church in America was established in the factory city of Lynn; Jesus was "the most famous and influential of all workingmen," its founder declared. John Boyle O'Reilly, the eminent poet and editor of Boston's influential Catholic newspaper the *Pilot*, wrote about an "irrepressible conflict" between the slaves of capitalism and its masters, and declared that socialism was "the hope of the people." The *Pilot*'s book review column responded enthusiastically to the work of a European writer named Karl Marx. The New England idyll was over.

But it wasn't over for the millowners or the mill agents and the superintendents who worked for them. Their political, religious, and social connections were unimpeachable. Often the owners lived in the mill towns, which they dominated completely, and ran the mills themselves. If they lived outside, in Providence, Boston, or New York, their representative in town was the mill agent, who usually lived in an ample Victorian, i.e., new, house supplied by the company. The mill agent's office was in the countinghouse, near where the hands lined up each Saturday afternoon to get their wages. (Usually they were paid in cash, but sometimes the pay was scrip which could be spent only at the company store.) Outside the agent's office sat the clerks, who brought him orders for cloth received from the selling houses in Boston or New York and sent out letters ordering cotton or wool to make that cloth. Under the agent, at about half his salary, was the superintendent, the man who actually ran the mill. He too lived in an ample house supplied by the company, though not quite so fine a house as the agent's. Each morning he toured the entire mill to make sure that everything and everybody was working properly, that the cloth was of the proper quality, and that it was being woven fast enough. After lunch, he repeated his tour, checking with the foreman of each room to see how things were going. For it was the foreman who really oversaw production. He was the chief contact with the millhands; he hired and fired them and taught them how to run their machines.

Many of the millowners, agents, and superintendents had themselves worked in a mill at one time and, as the 1886 biography of a Rhode Island millowner says, were "obliged to forego educational advantages" and give their "boyhood years to toil in the cotton mill." The millowners were proud of having risen in the world, of having ingeniously made improvements in the machines on which their fortunes had been built; they were proud of having bought old mills or rebuilt them if they had burned down; they were proud of building "for the operatives . . . a considerable village of neat tenement houses" and giving money "toward the erection of a handsome edifice for the use of the Methodist Episcopal church." They were the ones who donated the libraries, the high schools, and the new town halls. They didn't dribble their money away on salaries for the operatives, but saved it up to buy solid buildings that would bear their names for eternity.

They were versatile and ingenious men, immensely self-satisfied and immensely pleased with their accomplishments and their products. One Worcester manufacturer, who produced a third of the iron and steel wire made in America in 1880, boasted that his wire "hangs in the window for the canary's cage, catches the fish and broils it, ticks in the clock . . . sings in the piano or the harp. . . . It pours upon the community a perpetual shower of buckles, tacks, bolts, screws, pins and needles." And in 1898 another manufacturer gave a speech congratulating himself mightily for having invented a machine that produced 110 horseshoe nails a minute, going through almost 2,000 separate operations. Smugly he pointed out that nails for horseshoes were constantly in demand; once used, they couldn't be used again, unlike the buttons he had formerly manufactured. Alas, his satisfaction was to be short-lived. Soon a new machine would replace the horse. Other shrewder manufacturers were proud of their diversification, like the head of one Connecticut company that made eggbeaters, can openers, twine holders, hooks and eyes, bird-cage hooks, picture hooks, coat hooks, pulleys, napkin rings, safety pins, pulls and roller ends for window shades, nutcrackers, sewing-machine needles, cupboard latches, drawer pulls, and that characteristic Connecticut product, the nutmeg grater. Nor was that the end of the list.

That company is still in operation and still prospering, as is another Connecticut company that once did a big business in scythes and that turned in the twentieth century to making fiberglass boats, and a Massachusetts company that once produced daguerreotype cases and now makes plastic toothbrushes. Most of the textile mills are gone, and shoes sold in New England are as likely to come from Europe and the Far East as from Brockton or Lynn. But a surprisingly large number of small companies have survived in the towns and mills that housed them a century ago. And the descendants of the workers who despaired of ever getting out of the mills are often still there too, in the same mills. But now they make plastic by the mile instead of textiles, electronic components rather than thumbtacks, and three hundred and fifty dollars a week rather than eight.

A proud owner introduces his crew at a Norwalk, Connecticut hat factory.

Shipbuilding was New England's first industry. Above, shipwrights put ribs to a keel in Newington, New Hampshire. At right is a busy Essex, Massachusetts shipyard.

Even well into the Industrial Age,
handcrafts continued. Above is a family of basketmakers
from Stamford, Connecticut. At right, a team of Maine coopers
displays the tools and products of their trade.

At left, a wheelwright works in his shop
at Shrewsbury, Massachusetts, around 1895.
Above, another Massachusetts artisan weaves a seat
for a chair that reproduces a Colonial period
New England design.

In Connecticut, workers stack new-made bricks for drying.
Until the 1880s, when invention of a hot-air oven made it possible to make bricks
in winter, brickyard workers were laid off for several months.

Not unemployment, but the awful stench was the hazard for tannery workers.
Curriers in Salem, Massachusetts, work outdoors to dissipate the smell.

Connecticut armories long supplied
the world's need for guns. At left, workmen hand-finish rifles
during World War I. Below, in the Remington Arms factory,
women inspect rifle cartridges.

In the 19th century, Waterbury, Connecticut
became Clock City. Above, ormolu mountings are prepared
for fancy mantle clocks. At right, workmen assemble
the diabolic machines that woke America up.

Coils of heavy steel wire
fill a factory yard outside Worcester,
Massachusetts' mammoth mill,
the American Steel and Wire Company.

On the following pages are some of the activities
that the company organized for
the safety and entertainment of its workers:
a fire department (above, left)
an orchestra (below, left),
a Christmas party (above, right),
and a patriotic pageant.

Within a decade of the invention of photography,
the handsome mill above, in Woodstock, Vermont, was immortalized.
Shortly after the Civil War, a small-town Rhode Island mill (right)
made its foremen, mechanics, and millgirls feel right
at home by putting curtains in the windows.

Millworkers' children find room to play
in a crowded tenement yard in Lynn, Massachusetts.

By about 1880,
the giant Amoskeag mills
dominated the town of
Manchester, New Hampshire.

The Amoskeag company provided
playgrounds and gardens for its workers' children,
expecting full well that they'd be laboring
more profitably inside the mills
in a few years.

On the final pages in this section, the Amoskeag mill
buildings stretch for more than a mile and a half
along the Merrimack River and its canals.

# VI.

# THE SCHOOLTEACHER

# OF AMERICA

Battered but unbowed, Yale's 1895 football team beat Harvard, Princeton, Pennsylvania, and Wesleyan, embarrassing the latter by 72 to 0.

On the preceding page, Wellesley seniors cooperatively spell out their year of graduation on the slope below College Hall.

In 1869, when the young Ohio author William Dean Howells returned home from Boston, he went to visit a friend and, sitting on the veranda, started to tell him about literary life in New England. "Just a minute," said the friend. "He ran down," Howells later wrote, "first to one fence and then to the other at the sides and waved a wild arm of invitation to the neighbors who were also sitting on their back porches. 'Come over here!' he shouted, 'He's telling about Holmes and Longfellow and Lowell and Whittier.' And at his bidding, dim forms began to mount the fences and follow him up to his veranda. 'Now go on,' he called to me, when we were all seated, and I went on . . . and the hours drew toward midnight."

For nineteenth-century America, New England was the seat of all culture. You couldn't shoot a gun in any direction in Cambridge without bringing down an author, said the western writer Bret Harte, a man who was accustomed to guns. Emerson lived in Concord; so did that immensely popular and learned author Louisa May Alcott and her father, the philosopher Bronson Alcott, who traveled around the country lecturing on New England writers. In Boston the famous Saturday Club met weekly with Longfellow, Lowell, Oliver Wendell Holmes, and lesser authors, gathering over a good meal to talk for hours; from time to time Emerson left Concord to travel into Boston to join them. One caustic observer called the Saturday Club "The Mutual Admiration Society," for New England authors had an immoderately high opinion of themselves. But the rest of the country shared that opinion, for New England wrote and published the books America read, and originated the ideas America thought, the way New York and California have done in the twentieth century.

New England was the schoolteacher of America. Its reformers led movements for the abolition of slavery and for improving the treatment of the insane. They tried to bring education to the deaf and to women, and they succeeded, and they led the Temperance Movement that was to conquer America with Prohibition. They encouraged the growth of public schools and founded colleges everywhere they went. It was a New England senator, Justin Morrill of Vermont, whose Land Grant Act fostered the establishment of state colleges, forming a foundation for higher education in the Midwest and West. New England's own college graduates were everywhere, and everywhere they promoted the glories of New England education and displayed the results. The president of Kalamazoo College in Michigan went to school in Vermont as did the first principal of the North Carolina Institute for the Deaf, Dumb, and Blind. New England came to be revered as a symbol of all that was good and pure in America, an ethnic treasury of W.A.S.P. life, before the term "White Anglo-Saxon Protestant" was coined.

"After God had carried us safe to New England, and we had builded our houses, provided necessaries for our livelihood, rear'd convenient places for God's worship, and settled the Civil Government, one of the next things we longed for, and looked after was to advance *Learning*," a Puritan writer reported in 1643. New England had the first public school in America, the still-flourishing Boston Latin School, and the first college. In the years after the Civil War, that college, Harvard, also became America's first university. Late in the nineteenth century, when upper-class Americans began to send their children away to boarding schools, as English aristocrats did, those boarding schools were built in New England—Groton, St. Paul's, Taft, and a dozen more for men, and a few for women as well. New England colleges attracted students from all over the country. By 1900 education was well on its way to becoming one of the great industries of New England.

Around 1870, under the influence of its new president Charles W. Eliot, Harvard began to modernize the traditional college curriculum. Before Eliot's reforms, Harvard students had to take elocution and ethics, Latin and Greek. Eliot gave them the option of studying instead such newly elevated subjects as chemistry, archaeology, and art history. Chapel attendance, which had been compulsory, now became optional. To get a degree, graduates of the medical school had been obliged to pass only five out of nine examinations. Now, fortunately for their patients, they were required to pass all nine. Eliot built a physics laboratory and gave students the opportunity to study to be architects. By 1890 Harvard students could choose from at least eighteen courses in Greek and thirteen in Semitic; they could study metallurgy, Iranian, and Roman law. The result was the professionalization of learning. Harvard established a graduate school to turn out specialists in various fields of scholarship, and other colleges in New England and throughout the country followed its lead.

Not all students cared, of course. Many were content to get a grade of C in their courses. Gentlemen weren't supposed to be grinds anyway. "Bully for Greece. There are no flies on Greece" was all that one Harvard student, attending a course on Greek art, could find to write in his lecture notes. By the end of the nineteenth century, Harvard undergraduates were divided neatly into two groups—those with money and social position and those without. The rich, a great many of them from New York, lived in lavish dormitories on a Cambridge street familiarly called the "Gold Coast." Other students lived in the old college halls in Harvard Yard, in rooms that had been good enough for Thoreau and Emerson but weren't good enough for New York society students. The rich kept pet dogs in their rooms and stabled their own polo ponies nearby; they joined exclusive dining clubs and spent their leisure time playing billiards or strumming the mandolin; they dressed nattily in the latest, hand-tailored London fabrics and gave their cast-off clothing to the Y.M.C.A. for "missionary work among colored people in Talladega, Alabama," as the Harvard *Crimson* reported in 1899. The less fashionable students studied and picked up a little cash tutoring classmates who needed extra help to earn their gentleman's C. A few students managed to combine both worlds. "Only one gentleman stands ahead of me academically," an undergraduate named Theodore Roosevelt boasted late in the 1870s. Of course many nongentlemen stood ahead of him, but they hardly counted in Roosevelt's circle. Although most Harvard students were not from rich or prominent families, they were a select group nevertheless. Around 1890 a year at college cost about twice as much as the average workingman's annual wages.

The more serious students might themselves join the Mandolin Club, but they were more likely to devote their efforts to ideas, to study, or to debates on such subjects as: Resolved, That it is a benefit to the United States to receive immigrants at the present rate. (President Eliot himself, they doubtless noted, was on the side of the affirmative. "The more Italian immigrants that come to the United States, the better," he once wrote.) Many students donated time and knowledge teaching at the Breadwinner's College in Boston's slummy North End to provide immigrants with the rudiments of education, or taught elementary English, Latin, or history, math, and shorthand to workingmen in poorer parts of Cambridge.

The other New England colleges were much smaller than Harvard. In 1886 Brown had a student body of 239 and a faculty of only 26, and that number included the president, who doubled, or perhaps it's fairer to say tripled, as Professor of Natural Theology and Moral and Intellectual Philosophy. Still, Brown was up-to-date enough so that students could study zoology, astronomy, physiology, analytical chemistry, and civil engineering, as well as the more traditional subjects. Around the same time Middlebury College in Vermont had only 38 students. Two decades later Bowdoin and Bates had about 400 students each and Wesleyan had about 300. But small numbers didn't mean that college life couldn't be lively or intellectually rich. By 1906 Wesleyan had a literary monthly, a scientific association, and seven fraternities, each of which maintained an elegant house. It also had a number of secret societies, one called Skull and Serpent and another called Corpse and Coffin, whose members posed for group pictures dressed in formal clothes and, ominously, holding skulls. It was great fun. There were a Glee Club, a Mandolin Club, and a club for graduates of Stamford High School and Brooklyn High School. There were the Sophomore Hop, the Junior Prom, and the Senior Ball; there were cross-country runs, and in winter the more adventurous boys skated more than fifteen miles up the frozen Connecticut River to visit girls in Hartford.

Even farther upriver, in Massachusetts, there were girls aplenty at Smith College and at Mount Holyoke. Mount Holyoke had been founded as a "Female Seminary" in 1837. But the first New England women's school worthy of being called a college was not established until 1875, when Sophia Smith gave money to build Smith College in Northampton, across the Connecticut River from Mount Holyoke. Its purpose was "to furnish women with the means of usefullness, happiness and honor now withheld from them." In the 1870s there had been many discussions about colleges turning coed. Amherst, Harvard, Yale, Williams, and Dartmouth all considered it, and newspaper editorials called for coeducation with the now-familiar argument that segregated education was inherently unequal. Although Boston University was founded as a coed school in 1869 and Wesleyan admitted women for several decades after 1875, separate but equal education won out. Smith and Wellesley were established in the 1870s for women only and the Society for the Collegiate Instruction of Women, later named Radcliffe, was founded at Harvard in 1879; among its founding mothers was Alice Longfellow—"grave Alice" of *The Children's Hour*, whose father was a Harvard professor as well as the nation's best-known poet.

"Great natural laws," wrote a physician opposing the establishment of any college for women, "make women between the ages of fifteen and forty-five essentially a separate and higher order of beings than men, destined for a purpose wholly feminine." That purpose wasn't study nor was it involvement with public affairs. Woman's place was in the home. "Women are too nervous and hysterical to enter politics," one nineteenth-century Massachusetts legislator edgily declared. They had to be protected, unless of course they were millworkers. As a result, although Smith girls followed a course of study no less rigorous than that at the "best New England colleges," as its prospectus announced, they had to go to bed by 10:00 P.M. and they had to take regular exercises in the gymnasium and out in the open air "under the direction of an educated lady physician."

Naturally many women disagreed with these assessments of their limitations. In the 1880s Wellesley College girls were regularly conducted on pilgrimages to visit the veteran women's rights leader Lucy Stone, who lived nearby with her husband, Henry Blackwell. As early as 1853, that couple had signed a marriage contract which provided for Lucy Stone to retain her own name, property, and earnings. Women were coming out of the kitchen closet and out of the colleges to enter journalism, law, and business, and to pioneer in a new profession—social work. In 1892 Smith alumnae founded a settlement house in the slums of Boston, where they tried to live just as the poorest workers did.

Of course those—male or female—who were able to attend college were very few. Many city students unable to afford the expense went to such institutions as the Schofield Commercial College or the Bryant and Stratton Business College, both in Providence, where they could master double-entry bookkeeping, commercial law, and correspondence and learn how to prepare that correspondence with proper penmanship or up-to-date typewriting. Or they could attend the Rhode Island School of Design, chartered in 1887, to learn drawing, painting, modeling, and design; then they could teach art themselves or get jobs with one of southern New England's flourishing jewelry or silver companies. In Worcester they could go to Foster's Business College, "a school for both sexes, unsurpassed in excellence," and in Boston in 1884 they had a choice of the Boston Telegraph Institute, four art schools, several business colleges, a conservatory of music, or the Massachusetts College of Pharmacy. There were also normal schools throughout New England run by the cities or the states to prepare young women to teach in the new primary schools, grammar schools, and high schools that were gradually replacing the old-fashioned district schools—the traditional one-room schoolhouses.

Their graduates, the schoolteachers, did not have an easy lot. Discipline was a problem because each teacher had to deal with an unmanageable number of children. In 1845 Cambridge, Massachusetts, teachers had to supervise seventy-one children in each class. By 1895 that figure had diminished to thirty-eight, but by then Cambridge was a very progressive city. Many towns still had awkwardly large classes; around the same time Boston, with its great tradition of leadership in public education, had fifty pupils in each primary-school class. In both urban and rural schools, attendance was erratic. "They are out of school at all seasons in all weather to weed, drop, set, hoe, worm, sucker, cut, hang, take down and strip tobacco," complained the school committee of the Connecticut River tobacco-growing town of Hadley, Massachusetts, in 1872. "Finished school today," a sixteen-year-old New Hampshire boy had written in his diary ten years earlier. "I have been to school 22 1/2 days, absent 1/2 day, tardy 2." Apparently, that wasn't enough time for him to learn sentence structure. That's the way it was out in the country. But even in the cities, where school attendance was more regular, parents kept children out of school to carry their father's dinner pail to the factory or to work in the factory themselves. In many mill towns school attendance was very low. Around 1870 almost half the children between five and fifteen stayed out of school in Lawrence and Salem, Massachusetts. In Lowell the tone was evidently a little more intellectual; only about a quarter of the children stayed home.

To deal with truancy, many industrial towns organized factory schools "in such a manner," as the authorities in one Massachusetts town put it, "as to cause the least inconvenience to employers and to parents who are dependent upon the labor of their children." In these "half-time schools," children attended classes three hours a day for forty weeks, while working in the mills three-fourths of the time for an entire year and receiving full pay from their charitable employers. The children saw school as a little vacation from work and their parents, who lived in an age when children were thought to owe their parents more than their parents owed them, were happy too since their children brought in a full income. Soon after the Civil War, Boston newsboys were gathered off the streets and sent to special schools for two hours in the morning to be taught the three R's, morals, and good manners; their hours were carefully timed so they wouldn't interfere with business. And for those factory workers who had never gone to school or who had just come to America, the cities established evening schools which taught reading, writing, and English, "thereby aiding in amalgamating the races," the Boston School Committee proclaimed around 1900. In the words of one factory agent, millhands who only "made their mark" on the payroll in November but who learned to write their names after a few months of evening school, "stood three inches higher in their boots."

In rural regions one-room schoolhouses lingered well into the twentieth century. Many of their teachers, unable to afford room and board at the normal schools, had to rely on the Teachers' Institutes that were held periodically in rural towns, where traveling professors lectured to the yokels on how to do it properly. But it took more than a college degree to teach in a one-room schoolhouse. The teacher sat alone on a platform near the entrance door next to a pile of wood for the fire. Her students sat beneath her on backless benches ranged on three sides of the room, with the youngest sitting in the middle. When the big boys came back to school in winter, when there were few farm chores to do, the benches got crowded; inevitably there were unruly scenes when younger children were pushed off the edge of a bench, or pretended to have been pushed off; and throughout the year the small children sitting in the middle of the room loudly voiced their resentment whenever the older children used their seats or their backs as footrests. Not much learning went on.

Reform of the district school system brought graded schools, where children were separated by age or level of learning, though parents complained that this segregated siblings from each other. But grading was the modern way. Cities and towns were proud of their graded primary schools and grammar schools, and of their new high schools, which prepared a few children for college or for success in the business world. The most up-to-date towns even had kindergartens, such as one in Connecticut in 1892 where children gathered daily on little red chairs in a sunny bay window, sang songs, "became acquainted with their bird neighbors," and listened to, or at least heard, talks on "Right Living and Patriotism." Most children never went either to kindergarten or to high school though. They contented themselves with graduating from grammar school, which was considered an accomplishment, or they left school as soon as they could, often before the legal school-leaving age of fifteen. By that age, one Massachusetts school committee declared more than a century ago, every boy or girl "ought to have acquired the rudiments of a good education"; but many were "unable to read fluently easy English prose; still more could hardly dare attempt to write a letter of business or friendship; cannot perform . . . simple operations in arithmetic, and are almost ignorant of the physical and political geography of our own land." Johnny couldn't read or write, they complained a hundred years ago, and they blamed it on the crude influences of rural life. Johnny still can't read and write, and now the blame falls on television and teachers' unions. A century from now no doubt there'll be a different reason.

Wellesley girls studied their chemistry with care, as well as their choices of lab smocks.

In 1882, Wellesley mathematicians boned up on their solid geometry
with Miss Helen Shafer, later President of the College.

Art instruction was a regular part of the curriculum at Ivy League schools.

Above, women were apparently admitted to the studio at Yale, though not matriculated at the College.

At right, Smith students work from a properly clad male model.

In the 1860s, the two Yalies at left
found lounging robes well suited for studying.
No mere clotheshorse, however, the man with his feet up,
John W. Sterling, made a huge fortune and left
15 million dollars of it to his alma mater.

The scene below reveals that formal headgear
was evidently required when the Brown class of 1875
played cards.

On the following pages, daily headwear
at Brown (left) and Yale (right)
featured the derby hat.

Above, Smith athletes do a vigorous-looking push-up.

At left, on May Day in 1899, Wellesley girls perform the ancient ritual
of hoop-rolling.

On the following pages,
Dartmouth's big wheels decide which way to go.

At left, Harvard's '88 tug-of-war team lies down on the job. Above, no sooner had James Naismith invented basketball (as a non-contact antidote to football) than a 1904 Smith team was polishing its zone defense.

History relates that the oarsmen
pictured at right are Harvard's heavyweight crew.
The tonnage of Wellesley's 1882 rowing team (above)
is unrecorded.

The green at Hanover, New Hampshire served as a baseball diamond

when the Big Green team of Dartmouth met Boston University.

Tradition and ceremony played key roles at Ivy League colleges—to build school spirit
and encourage group participation.
At left, Wellesley undergraduates frolic on Tree Day in 1902.
Above, Smith students celebrate Ivy Day.

Yale's famous singers, the Whiffenpoofs,
masquerade as contemporary notables in front of Mory's,
the eating club that they made famous.

Many students majored in fun. Above, Yale men go berserk.

On the following pages, a yardful of Harvardians attempts sobriety.

# VII.
# IN THE CITIES

Beside Boston Common an apple seller plied her trade; fronting the park
is Beacon Street, seen on the preceding page.

In one year during the 1880s more than sixteen thousand people were arrested for drunkenness in Boston and thirteen were arrested for smoking opium. One person was nabbed for unlawfully extinguishing streetlamps and another for distributing obscene material. The city had shopbreakers and arsonists, rapists and pickpockets and even polygamists. It was a big city, having more than doubled in size in little over two decades, and quadrupled in size in the previous forty years. The population was almost four hundred thousand. Bostonians liked to think of their city as unique, but in many ways it was not. The growth of cities was one of the most striking phenomenons of the nineteenth century, not only in America but in Europe as well. Great industrial centers were rising there too. Just as New England farmers did, European peasants who didn't emigrate to America left their homes to move to cities where life was a bit easier and money more plentiful.

Boston had all the problems of a big city, but it had all the modern advantages, too. Although the immigrants and their offspring lived in slum cellars, the city also had fine mansions in the Back Bay and on Beacon Hill and one suburb, Brookline, that was considered to be the richest town in the world. It had street after street of new two- and three-family houses, where sober workingmen lived, raising their families comfortably and sending their neatly dressed children off to school each day. The city had famous historic sites — Faneuil Hall and the Common and the Old State House, which was actually almost new, since it had been restored to its pristine condition in 1882 after having been rented out for years as business premises. It had public-spirited and wealthy citizens who supported a new Museum of Fine Arts, opened in 1876, and a symphony orchestra, established in 1881. In that same year some of these citizens banded together to found the Bostonian Society "to promote the study of the history of Boston, and the preservation of its antiquities." It was they who restored the Old State House, after saving it from progressives who wanted to tear it down to widen the streets around it.

It was true that Boston's streets needed widening. They were narrow and crowded, and traffic on them was intolerably bad. And so the city opened the nation's first subway in 1897, and topped that off by constructing one of the world's largest railroad stations. Fine new boulevards were built throughout the city, with trolley lines running along them, and a bicycle track was laid out over which members of the League of American Wheelmen might speed. In 1889 the first electric-powered trolley appeared in Boston, making obsolete the horsecars that had served Bostonians for so many years; and on Christmas Day, 1900, the last horsecar in the city rumbled down a Back Bay street. With the coming of the trolley, ordinary Bostonians who lived in outlying sections of the city could travel "in town," as they said, to gawk at the splendid new mansions built on the reclaimed tidal flats of the Back Bay, the residences of other, less ordinary Bostonians whose ancestors had had the cash and the foresight to invest in the China trade or in the early textile mills. They could stroll on the Common or promenade among the parterres of the Public Garden, "the gem of the city parks," as one guidebook called it, "a flower garden with rich verdure, a dainty foil to the plainer Common." For a time the Public Garden was a not-so-respectable gem; but it became respectable again after its well-wooded lakeside peninsula, notorious as a resort for excessively passionate lovers' trysts, was reformed by being made into an inaccessible island. Trolleys also carried Bostonians outside the city, to beaches set aside as public reservations, to parklike riverbanks and hills, and to vast forested tracts where lovers could, if they wanted to, tryst undisturbed.

Boston had hospitals, colleges, and theaters and what an 1883 report called "the most efficient and largest police force of any city in the country." It had a Home for Intemperate Women, a Home for Aged Women, a Home for Aged Colored Women, a Penitent Females' Refuge, and dozens of other charities, for Bostonians were notoriously high-minded. "It has ever been Boston's creed to render life safer and happier for the coming generation," as Helen Keller once wrote. Among the charities were many established by immigrants to aid distressed compatriots. There was one for Italians and another for Swiss, and still others for Portuguese, Norwegians, and French-speaking Belgians, but none apparently for Flemish-speaking Belgians. It had businessmen's clubs and workingmen's associations, including one quaintly called the Knights of the Wrench. It had more than six hundred licensed stores where the city's sixteen thousand criminal drunkards could purchase liquor and a good many unlicensed ones too, which escaped the vigilance of the nation's best police force; but as if to compensate, it also had a Moral Reform Society, a Temperance Alliance, a Temperance Society, a Total Abstinence Society, and the Women's Christian Temperance Union.

Other smaller New England cities imitated Boston as best they could. Lynn's factory workers enjoyed the use of the nation's second largest city park—two thousand acres in size—and in Providence, a descendant of Roger Williams donated parkland on Williams's old farm on the outskirts of the city. The famous architect of Boston's great Trinity Church, H.H. Richardson, was kept busy with commissions for railroad stations and courthouses in other cities. Like Boston, all the New England cities had been growing throughout the nineteenth century. Streets were paved, water supplies improved, sewer systems built, and arrangements made for the regular removal of garbage. Boards of health were established, municipal ambulance services were started, and new hospitals were opened. Modern fire engines were purchased, and fire alarm boxes and hydrants erected at street corners. To make sure that plumbers were competent, cities began to examine them, and, once electricity arrived, they examined electricians too. In the 1880s cities began granting franchises to companies that would, for a fee, build and maintain electric light poles and wires. The lights often flickered because wires ran among trees and the generators were feeble, but by the end of the century, electricity had improved greatly and the streets were well lit. The use of electricity in homes, Cambridge reported in 1896, "is rapidly on the increase and most of the new dwellings are equipped with electric wiring." New England's second city, Providence, built new waterworks in 1871 and in the same year started the construction of modern sewers; a few years later it appointed an inspector of buildings to make sure that all factories and office buildings had fire escapes and that all new structures were properly built.

Proper construction was often more an ideal than a reality. Throughout New England in many overgrown mill towns enormous barracks like wooden three- and four-decker tenements housed workers newly arrived from Europe or Quebec. All of them were shoddily built, and some were so close together that even a garbage pail wouldn't fit between them. Their rooms were dark, small, and crowded, and they were firetraps. Some housed as many as two hundred residents, with only two or three doors allowing exit in case of fire. Jumping out of a window to escape a fire was often as dangerous as trying to get through the door; only a few feet separated buildings and fires easily spread from one to the other. In some of the tenements waste water from sinks ran into the yards, covering them with green slime. People lived, and drew their own water, in basements three feet below yard level.

Cities made valiant attempts to deal with growth, but it was often a losing battle. In 1876 Lawrence ensured itself a steady water supply through the construction of a modern pumping plant which piped Merrimack River water throughout the city. Unfortunately before the Merrimack reached Lawrence, the sewage of Manchester and Nashua in New Hampshire, and of Lowell ten miles upstream, emptied into it, along with chemicals from their textile mills. After 1893, when the river water was chemically purified, Lawrence's death rate dropped dramatically. Epidemics were a constant danger. In the 1870s the Board of Health in Holyoke, Massachusetts, had to inoculate every resident against smallpox. Typhoid fever appeared again and again in the crowded tenements with devastating effect. It didn't attack only the poor: the social season at Bar Harbor was ruined by an outbreak of the disease in 1873, and several Yale students died of it in New Haven in 1889.

As the years went on, the slums became increasingly crowded. Thousands of new immigrants arrived each year, many of them in response to a specific invitation by a New England millowner. Around the turn of the century, the port of Boston admitted thirty thousand annually. By that time, as a result of their presence, New England's old traditions seemed less and less dominant. Most New Englanders were now city dwellers and Catholics; Congregationalists, the heirs of the Puritans who had founded New England, had become a small minority. "I feel that we Yankees are as much a thing of the past as any race can be," one Boston writer complained in 1893. In no New England state did Catholics form less than half of the population and in one state, Rhode Island, almost three-fourths of the inhabitants were Catholic.

The immigrants had not had an easy time of it since the first great wave of Irish newcomers arrived as a result of the potato famine of the 1840s. Active persecution of the Irish ended before the Civil War, but even as late as 1890 no Boston bank would hire an Irish clerk. Until the 1880s Catholics in Massachusetts's charitable institutions and prisons had to attend Protestant services if they wanted to pray; no Catholic chaplains were allowed in. Rich Yankee boys on Beacon Hill or in Cambridge enjoyed nothing more than a fight with the Irish boys who lived in the nearby slums; of course the Irish boys enjoyed it too.

During the 1870s the Irish began rising in Boston politics, and by the next decade the city had its first Irish mayor, Hugh O'Brien, who boasted that Puritan Boston had become "the most Catholic city in the country." There were Irish aldermen and Irish police commissioners. The Common Council had two members named Lynch and two named Murphy, and a Donovan, a Donnelly, and a Doherty. A different Murphy and a different Doherty were members of the School Committee, although the Irish had expended immense efforts and immense sums to build their own parochial schools and colleges, where their children wouldn't be exposed to the insults to the Catholic religion that appeared in so many public school textbooks.

The Irish had had a difficult struggle to attain political power; once they won it, they enjoyed it. Mayor O'Brien shocked Protestant Bostonians by closing the public library to celebrate St. Patrick's Day. Eventually, however, the Irish had to share political power with other immigrants as Italians, Jews, French Canadians, and Poles began arriving in the decades before and after 1900. Many cities had an Irish ward and a French ward, and Italian and German precincts. In Lawrence, French Canadian voters were offended when they were addressed in English rather than in their own language. Lowell had a growing colony of Greeks whose coffee shops, with trays of baklava in the windows, intrigued the children of earlier immigrants and whose votes intrigued already established politicians. Armenians by the hundreds came to Worcester, where many found work in the wire factories. New Haven became a predominantly Italian city, and Poles settled along the Connecticut River in southern New England. Very soon the new immigrants were voters. Some Irish politicians, most notably John F. Fitzgerald, after whom an even more notable politician, his grandson John F. Kennedy, was named, were able to ride the tide of the new immigration and remain in power. Fitzgerald, who lived in a section of Boston where Nova Scotians, Jews, and, increasingly, Italians lived alongside the Irish, managed to become mayor of Boston and the founder of one of America's greatest political dynasties. Other politicians were not so successful.

The new immigrant groups produced their own politicians and their own newspapers, schools, churches, and organizations as well. In Boston, immigrants established German-speaking lodges of the Independent Order of Red Men; one was named after a local chief, Massasoit, and another after an overseas chief, Bismarck. In Providence in the 1880s, a bishop born in Ireland officiated in the cathedral and many other churches were led by Irish priests; but the city also had a French Catholic church, a Portuguese Catholic church, and a church with a largely Italian membership, and separate societies of German Catholics and black Catholics. The German Catholics "are not yet numerous or wealthy enough to build a church," a contemporary writer reported, taking it for granted that any ethnic group would build its own church as soon as it could. For even in the new land, ties to the old land remained strong. Many immigrants went back and forth to Europe several times before they finally settled in New England for good. Boston's Chinese merchants paid for Sun Yat-sen's return home to overthrow the Manchu emperor of China in 1911, and it was Boston Albanians who sewed the flag that was raised when Albania became independent in 1912.

The New England of the twentieth century was taking shape, a largely urban collage of ethnic enclaves suspicious of each other and of the Yankees, a place where Irish Catholic orphans were sheltered at one orphanage and French Catholic orphans at another. When the Beacon Hill boys stopped having snowball fights with Irish slum kids, the rich boys' place was taken by Italians; annually, almost religiously, there was a fierce gang rumble between the North End Italians and the Irish who lived nearby. The older inhabitants looked down on the newcomers. Although some do-gooders took immigrant boys to see the Bunker Hill Monument and the tomb of Cotton Mather, that persecutor of witches, to teach them about the glories of their New England heritage, many despaired of assimilating the immigrants. "The Irish race," declared Charles Francis Adams, the scion of another of America's great political dynasties, "have as few elements in common with the native New Englander as one race of men well can have with another." The Irish in turn looked down on the Italians, the French, the Greeks, and the Jews—all of whom fortunately had each other to look down on.

But some people were optimistic about the future. "What is it in New England," one writer rather patronizingly asked in 1911, "that takes the dregs of Europe and makes not only good citizenship of it, but makes of it good physical manhood?" These were some of the dregs: Angelo Cazassa, Mariano Coppolino—fruit dealers; Jacob Schwartz, M. Levine—tailors; Michæl Corcoran, John McCarthy—teamsters. The dregs of Asia joined them: Hop Ching, Lee Yuen—laundrymen; and so did hundreds of thousands of others. New England's city directories were filled with their names along with the names of the Nickersons, Ballous, Curtises, and Pierces who had preceded them to the land of that once independent red man, Massasoit. They crowded each other on the trolleys and jostled each other in the streets, and their children sat beside each other in the schools and worked beside each other in the factories and office buildings of New England. Eventually, late in the twentieth century, they would even befriend each other.

Bridgeport, Connecticut's citizens turned out in force
for a World War I parade down Main Street.

By the first quarter of the 20th century,
the downtowns of Waterbury, Connecticut (above) and Lynn, Massachusetts (left)
were already buzzing with traffic.

A big event in every city was the annual circus parade.
Opposite, elephants march two by two in Stamford, Connecticut.
Above, in 1910, children chase a clown from the Adam Forepaugh and
Sells Brothers Circus down the main drag of Lewiston, Maine.

Boston Harbor, busiest in New England,
still saw ships under sail well into modern times.

Boston's Mount Vernon Street was, and is, a fashionable address.

A lovely, linear park graces Commonwealth Avenue in Boston.

Town and gown came together at
the water fountain on New Haven's central Green (right).

Below, in Norwalk, Connecticut, soon after
the outbreak of war in 1914, a taxi driver
patriotically shows the flag.

Overleaf: the blizzard of '88 gave
New Haven's State Street shopkeepers
plenty of exercise.

Immigrant laborers
did much of the heavy work
in New England's growing cities.
Above, a crew in western Massachusetts works
on a sewer line.

At right,
Irish navvies fix up a railroad bridge
in Brattleboro, Vermont.

Above, horsedrawn carts laden with produce
rumble through Boston's busy Haymarket Square.
At right, horseless wagons brought meat, fish,
and produce to Frank Jessup's customers
in Stamford, Connecticut.

A grocery store in Dover, New Hampshire
is all decked out for a patriotic celebration.

Department stores replaced the specialty shops in larger cities
of old New England before the turn of the century.

Above, a large housewares store in Barre, Vermont,
sold all the bric-a-brac a Victorian home could wish.

Ladies try on gloves at Forbes and Wallace in Springfield, Massachusetts.

This bartender of Dover,
New Hampshire, stood ready
to quench the thirsts of workers
in the city's cotton mills.

On the following pages
is Dover's poolhall where,
as signs on the wall indicate,
players occasionally tried to sneak
a free game or hustle
a buck or two.

Movie theatres in Providence (above)
and Boston (right) offered diversions at five or ten cents.
Costlier, but more uplifting, was the fare at Waterville,
Maine's opera house (below).

Boston's Museum of Fine Arts, founded in 1870,
offered visitors an extraordinary range of ancient and recent
works of art.

Ethnic food and music were sold
on city streets: above and below are
Boston merchants; at right,
a hurdy-gurdy man poses in Lynn,
Massachusetts.

Not far from elegant Beacon Street,
in a squalid alley,
Boston's immigrant children play
the great American game.

Above, Boston mayor John F. ("Honey Fitz") Fitzgerald makes friends handing out Christmas
baskets at Salvation Army headquarters. Fitzgerald was elected by fellow Irish-Americans,
like the worker at right who confronts a top-hatted Brahmin during a labor dispute. In 1909
Fitzgerald won re-election so narrowly that a recount at Faneuil Hall (above, right) was required.

Overleaf: the wave of the future was clear as Boston workers, like others, rallied together.

# Acknowledgments

Jane Sugden and Norman Kotker wish to thank all the people from New England whose cooperation and assistance made this book possible. Jane Sugden would especially like to acknowledge the following: Andreas Brown; David Freund; Rachel Keniston, Plymouth, N.H.; Edith LaFrancis; Marius Péladeau; Ellie Reichlin and David Bohl (Society for the Preservation of New England Antiquities); Marie and Joseph Sugden, Trumbull, Conn.; Maureen Taylor (Rhode Island Historical Society); Lillian Thayer; Louise Tullis, Rangeley, Me.; and Alice Waldecker (Norfolk Historical Society); and to express particular gratitude to Claire Kelleher, Winchester, Mass., who helped with the photo research.

# Photographic Credits

*The photographer's name, if known, is given in italics.*

Robert J. Adsit family, Burlington, Vt., 160, *Alvaro Adsit;* Aldrich Public Library, Barre, Vt., 99, 100 — 101, 278; Annisquam Historical Society, Donald K. Usher Coll., Mass., 56, 67, *Martha Hale Harvey;* Ashfield Historical Society, Mass., 23, 120 bot., *Howes Brothers;* Mildred Barnes, Essex Junction, Vt., 135; Margaret Bennett Coll., Fort Davis, Tex., 93; Bettmann Archive, New York City, 171; Boothbay Region Historical Society, Me., 43 top; Boston Public Library, Print Dept., 251; Bostonian Society, Old State House, Boston, 252, 285, 288; Brandon Free Public Library, Vt., 163 bot., *J.H. Cross;* Brattleboro, Vt., from *Before Our Time,* copyright 1974 by Harold A. Barry, Richard E. Michelman, Richard M. Mitchell, and Richard H. Wellman, published by Stephen Greene Press, Brattleboro, Vt., reproduced by permission of the authors, 273; Andreas Brown, Gotham Book Mart, New York City, 37 bot., 136 bot.; Brown Brothers, Sterling, Pa., 48, 75, 104, 111, 198, 199, 200, 201; Brown University Archives, 231; Jane Lougee Bryant and Arthur Townsend Lougee, Limerick, Me., 131, *Frank Charles Philpot;* Canterbury Historical Society, N.H., 136 top, *Luther Cody;* Circus World Museum, Baraboo, Wis., 263; Frank Claes, Orland, Me., 172; Colby College Art Museum, 29, 34, *Chansonetta Stanley Emmons;* Connecticut Historical Society, Hartford, 77, 196; Connecticut State Library, Pictorial Archives, Mills Coll., Hartford, 123, 137; Corbit's, Bridgeport, Conn., 259, *Lewis H. Corbit;* Cotocheset Enterprises, Osterville, Mass., 127 bot.; Culver Pictures, New York City, 9; 20 — 21, 38, 41, 166 center, *Chansonetta Stanley Emmons;* 182, 189; Dartmouth College Library, 157, 161, 236 — 37; 242 — 43, *H.H.H. Langill;* Dorothy Dunn, Stamford, Conn., 275; Essex Institute, Salem, Mass., 197; Farmington Museum Coll., Conn., 116, *Karl Klauser;* George A. Farnum, Wilton, Me., 45 top; David Freund, Brooklyn, N.Y., 25, 81 bot., 140, 141; Edmund Gillon, Jr., New York City, 50 bot.; Hadley Historical Society, Mass., 122; Harvard University Graduate School of Business Administration, Baker Library, Boston, 202 — 3, 204, 205; Harvard University Archives, 238, 241, 248 — 49; Historically Speaking, Boston, 146, 264 — 65; 274, *Orville Rand;* Houghton Mifflin Co., Boston, from *Brahmins & Bullyboys* by Stephen Halpert and Brenda Halpert, photographs by *G. Frank Radway,* published by Houghton Mifflin Co., copyright 1973 by Stephen Halpert and Brenda Halpert, reprinted by permission, 292, 293, 294 — 95; International Museum of Photography at George Eastman House, Rochester, N.Y., 206; 290 — 91, *Lewis Hine;* Camp Kehonka, Wolfeboro, N.H., 167; Edith LaFrancis, Agawam, Mass., 26, 30, 96 — 97, 126 top, 272, *Howes Brothers;* Library of Congress, 4 — 5, *George Tingley;* 76; 208 — 9, *Frances B. Johnston;* University of Lowell, Special Coll., 181; Lumberman's Museum, Patten, Me., 80, 82, 86, 88 — 89; Lynn Historical Society, Mass., 114, 117 top, 118, *J.W. Darcy;* Madison Historical Society, Conn., 28, 175; Maine Historical Society, Portland, 70 — 71; Maine State Library, Draper Coll., Augusta, 90 right; Maine State Museum, Augusta, 24, 84 — 85, 92, 134; University of Maine at Orono, The Northeast Archives of Folklore and Oral History, 83; 90 left, *George Hallowell;* University of Maine at Orono, Raymond H. Fogler Library, Special Coll., 81 top, 87; Manches-ter Historic Association, N.H., 162, 210 — 11, 212, 213, 214 — 15; Mansfield Historical Society, Conn., 1; Peter Marcinek, Killingworth, Conn., 31, *Arthur Daniels;* McArthur Public Library, Biddeford, Me., 49; Museum of Fine Arts, Boston, 286, 287; Nantucket Historical Association, Mass., 170; New Hampshire Historical Society, Concord, 156; University of New Hampshire, Isle of Shoals Coll., Dept. of Media Services, Durham, 174; New Haven Colony Historical Society, Conn., 51, 145, 178 — 79, 269, *T.S. Bronson;* 270 — 71, *George R. Bradley;* Newfields Public Library, N.H., 113; Newport Historical Society, Me., 163 top; Norfolk Historical Society, Conn., 10, 22, 35, 120 top, 121 bot., 132 — 33, *Marie Kendall;* Northampton Historical Society, Mass., 138, 139; Norwalk Historical Reference Library, Lockwood House, Conn., 268, *Clarence Arnold;* Old Gaol Museum, York, Me., 27, 32; 66, *George Henry Donnell;* Peabody Museum of Salem, Mass., 55 left, 64, 65, 73, 78 — 79; 191, *George Wood;* Peacham Historical Association, Vt., 39; Marius B. Péladeau and Samuel Pennington Coll., Warren, Me., 19, *Chansonetta Stanley Emmons;* Daniel Perkins, Dover, N.H., 280 — 81, 282 — 83; Plymouth Historical Society, N.H., 91; Pocumtuck Valley Memorial Association, Deerfield, Mass., 42, 43 bot., 112, *Frances and Mary Allen;* Putney Historical Society, Vt., 33, 47; Rangeley Library Association, Me., 6, 165; Tyler Resch, Bennington, Vt., 94; Rhode Island Historical Society, Providence, 68, 115, 121 top, 169, 177, 207, 232, 284 top, back endpaper; Allie Ryan, South Brooksville, Me., 193; Sanford Historical Committee, Me., 119, 126 bot., 130; Millard Simpson, Cary, Me., 37 top, *Isaac Simpson;* Smith College Archives, 229, 235, 239, 245; Society for the Preservation of New England Antiquities, Boston, 46 top, *William S. Appleton;* 154, 155, 168, *N.L. Stebbins;* 158 — 59, 176; 194, *William Parker;* 195, 266, *Baldwin Coolidge;* 267; South Berwick Historical Society, N.H., 190; South Londonderry Library, Vt., 117 bot., *Everett Vaile;* Springfield City Library, Local History Dept., Mass., 279; Stamford Historical Society, Conn., 192, 262; Jane Stevens, Bath, Me., courtesy of Bond Wheelwright Co., Freeport, Me., 173, *James Perkins;* Tales of Cape Cod, Hyannis, Mass., 69; Lillian Thayer, Williamsville, Vt., 44, 46 bot., 50 top, *Porter Thayer;* Mr. and Mrs. Robert Tucker, Tunbridge, Vt., 52 — 53; Vermont Historical Society, Montpelier, front endpaper, *Will Chandler;* 45 bot., 95; 127 top, *Adelbert Corser;* Vermont Marble Co., Proctor, Vt., 98; University of Vermont, Bailey/Howe Library, Wilbur Coll., 36, *Tennie Gaskill Toussaint;* Walpole Historical Society, N.H., 142 — 43; Waterbury Republican & American, Conn., 261; Waterville Historical Society, Me., 284 bot.; Robert Weichert, Bennington, Vt., 40, 124 — 25, 164; Wellesley College Archives, 217, 226, 227, 234, 240, 244; Wenham Historical Association & Museum, Warren, Conant Coll., Mass., 118, *Benjamin H. Conant;* Whaling Museum, Old Dartmouth Historical Society, New Bedford, Mass., 72; 74, *Joseph G. Tirrell;* Robert Whitehouse, Dover, N.H., 276 — 77; Woodstock Historical Society, Vt., 2 — 3, 103, 128 — 29; Wyonegonic Camps, Denmark, Me., 166 top, 166 bot.; Yale University Archives, 218, 228, 230; 233, *T.S. Bronson;* 246, 247.

On the endpaper, at the Royal Weaving Company in Pawtucket, Rhode Island, millgirls tend a forest of skein-winding machines.